INTRODUCTION

For so many years the age old question has been, **"What do women want?"** The black woman is exceptional in the stride for the perfect relationship because she possesses so much more spiritual passion and is blessed with an inner-strength that sets her apart from the rest. *"To Love The Soul Of A Black Woman"* will take you on a reality ride with a philosophical twist.

"Once you learn how to make love to a black woman without touching her you are delving into the deepest depths of her soul. Have you ever experienced or heard of someone just start crying right in the middle of sex? I have... And when asked what's wrong, the answer is simply, "I just love you so much!" That's when you know you're making love to her soul and no amount of physical penetration can ever compare to that" jb brown

To love the soul is to love her mind, which produces the thoughts that generates and controls her actions. Therefore, to accept her actions is to understand her thoughts, hence embracing her mind, which clears the pathway to loving her soul.

There are no height, weight, or gender requirements to read this book. You just have to be sure that you can handle the truth!

D. Jerome Brown

PREFACE

There are no innocent people in this book, so the names have been changed to save face. If anyone is offended, embarrassed or otherwise defamed in any way, I apologize in advance for your moments of discomfort. No one is above reproach and the real person that the story depicts is a true inspiration to those who knows her. I pray that millions will grow from the education gained from reading this book. I'm giving it to you from first-hand experience; up close and personal; the hardcore, unfiltered, 100% reality and truth… Although it somewhat centers around one relationship it has the dynamics that will undoubtedly reach many others. There is just simply no way around it; in order to love the entrée you have to like the ingredients. A dish is not created to suit just one individual.

DEDICATION

This book is dedicated first and far most to God, who has implanted in me the talent and ability to continue to write. I have faced many pitfalls in my life and walked on the edge of destruction, yet still I keep resurfacing attempting to reach people once again. Secondly, I dedicate this book to my late parents, Mr. & Mrs. Edgar and Eunice Brown, who were the vessels that served as the pathways of my existence. Thirdly, it's dedicated to my children, of which will remain unnamed for their protection as they did not request to be on this earth and certainly didn't ask to be my off springs. Lastly, I dedicate it to the woman that inspired it, also to remain unnamed.

Though the time and elements shall keep us apart, you will always be with me here in my heart. I know that our paths didn't keep us together, but that's my fault, I couldn't stand the bad weather. Whoever shall have you will accomplish the goal of learning to love a true black woman's soul.
D. Jerome Brown

BIBLIOGRAPHY

Brown began writing poetry and short stories at age 12, then moved on to music at 19. Took an interest in acting and performing and ventured on to reach the honor of directing and acting with television's long time veteran, Sherman Hemsley, of "The Jefferson's." Has also written, produced and directed 5 independent movies, "Thy Will Be Done," "Ultimate Alibi," "Closing Statement" "Forbidden Love" and "Deception," which is five of eight movie scripts as well as 6 stage-plays.

He is an Ex-Theatre Professor at Life University College in Marietta. He also made several appearances on television's, "Walker, Texas Ranger," starring Chuck Norris and Clarence Guilyard. Brown's book, THINK NOT; THOUGHT NOT is a reflection of his life and experiences combined with other lives he's touched, encountered or witnessed. The book explores all genres ranging from and including inspiration, family, romance, humor, tragedy, and sorrow. The book is written in memory of his father, Edgar T. Brown. 03/15/30-07/21/02 The inventor and owner of, "Sur-Cap," a Glow In The Dark safety cap used to identify bottles from others.

TABLE OF CONTENTS

TLTSBW contains 10 lessons that I've learned throughout my life and 10 discussion questions that are brought to a monumental milestone of knowledge. Armed with this intelligence you too can love the soul of a black woman; the way she was meant to be loved.

LESSONS LEARNED

LESSON I   --- EMPTY YOUR BUCKET

LESSON II   --- NO UNFOUNDED STATEMENTS

LESSON III   --- KNOW WHAT YOU'RE DEALING

LESSON IV   --- BE RIGHTEOUS; "ALL" RIGHT

LESSON V   --- DON'T TAKE AWAY YOUR KINDNESS

LESSON VI   --- YOU CAN THROW A

FEATHER

LESSON VII   --- WHAT'S THE VALUE

LESSON VIII   --- OLD ROOTS BARE FRUITS

LESSON IX   --- THE TIME TO PREPARE FOR WAR

LESSON X   --- FAST IS TOO FURIOUS

CHAPTER I

"SHALL WE GROW TOGETHER"

Proverbs 23:7

King James Version (KJV) 7 "For as he thinketh in his heart, so is he: Eat and drink, saith he to thee; but his heart is not with thee." Ladies, let's talk about trust and faith! The number one response to the question, "what do you want from your man?" is, "For him to be honest and faithful." The first thing that comes to mind when we talk about trust is sex, creeping and being unfaithful; men think differently.

A person can be unfaithful without ever touching someone else. Men are expected to be strong, brave, provide and protect and that's okay. What you don't seem to keep in mind is we're still human. Men emerged from the same womb, sucked the same breast milk, and were held by the same loving arms of our Mothers as women were.

While it's okay for us to maintain that strong hero image in public, in private, sometimes we just simply need to be held, heard or hugged. The trust factor is, knowing that as our ladies, you will be there to hold us in our moment of weakness, without calling us weak, and thinking that we only have ulterior motives or just want sex.

Allow me to share my story with you about trust and faith or more specifically, how I violated it with several women for more than 31 years. First of all a big shout out to Facebook! 31 years ago I fell in love with a young lady, Wakina Webster, in Fayetteville, N.C. At 16, I cried like a little 3 year old child when my Mother forced me to go back to South Carolina and leave Wakina.

For 31 years I violated the trust and faith of every woman that I ever been with because I sustained Wakina's memory by constantly deploying the metaphysical portrayal of her being in my life. I kept her in my heart and mind, while subconsciously comparing her to every woman that I was ever with; wondering what it would be like if it was her.

I tried everything I could to find her. Resources were very limited back then. I ran away from home, I mailed letters to Fort Bragg, and I even joined the Army in the search for my then "true love." I ruined many relationships because I thought of her in my heart all those years.

Well guess what, I FOUND HER! I tried searching on Facebook in 2008 and gave up after no "no matches found." I decided to try it one more time in 2014 and she answered me. I bombarded her with questions about her Father, brother and where they lived, to confirm that it was her. Every response was correct! However, the one thing that rendered the greatest feeling of confirmation was the picture she had given me 31 years ago. A childhood bully had destroyed my picture of Wakina by scratching up her face with an ink pen. Now I can look him in his face and say, "Nanny, nanny, boo-boo! Wakina still had the original and texted me a copy!

I cannot describe the feeling that went through me as she and I shared information and learned that we both have two children, ages 26 and 19, boy and girl, we both joined the Army, we both went into the medical field, and we both sustained a head injury while in the military. And get this Facebook, she only lives 94 miles away from me, and has also been to Dobbins Air Force Base many times where I was stationed for 6 years!

Wakina shared one of the most powerful statements with me that I have ever heard from a woman. She said, **"I've never really felt like I've gotten back what I'm worth from a relationship."** It sent shivers through me. Only God knows if she and I portrayed so many similarities over the years because our souls were somehow connected. Talking to her after all those years gave me an incredible feeling of relief, as if I was imprisoned and walked out a free man. I have never disclosed those deeply rooted thoughts that I held on to for so long, with anyone.

Ladies, what men really want to know is can we trust you with our deepest thoughts and feelings. Why do you think we go to the strip clubs and open up to strippers, to bars or Hooters and hang out with the fellas? It's not just because we want to look at naked women; it's because we don't have faith and trust that you will take our deepest feelings and not hold them against us. Most men talk more in the hour that we sneak away to the strip club than we do an entire evening at home.

I admit that I was wrong for keeping Wakina's memory in my heart all those years and I know that I would have loved better, stronger and had been a better man and husband had

I not. I can't undo it and I can't take it back, but the closure from finding and talking to her has given me more strength and character than you could begin to imagine or I could begin to explain.

"To Love The Soul Of A Black Woman" delves deep into the depths of the black woman's life, body and soul, which is the mind. We'll talk more about that later. Many black women walk in blind faith and when a person adheres to that type of commitment it is hard if not impossible to make them deviate from that path.

When you learn to love the soul of a black woman you learn that becoming and staying in tune with her nucleus keeps her focused on the ultimate goal, which is pleasing and loving Jesus. She would rather exchange you than to change herself. The average black woman will not alter themselves or their faith to please a man. We have to know that the black women stay "prayed up," and their love for God is a prominent part of her daily thoughts.

The two most prominent words in the black woman's vocabulary are, "Praise God!" A black woman can find a pair of shoes that fit or a purse that matches her outfit and she will say praise God, so somebody tell me why does a person challenge a woman's faith by thinking that if they cheat and get caught it gives them more leverage if they say, **"GOD KNOWS I NEVER MEANT TO HURT YOU?"** Doesn't God know everything anyway?

We were created of our own free will and just because you say he knows I didn't mean to hurt you doesn't give you a free pass, He didn't "will" you to cheat! Perhaps you meant, "God knows I didn't mean to get caught!"

Some men are extremely confused as to what aspects of a woman constitute acknowledging the soul. Have you ever observed how men will sit up erect and take notice of a beautiful woman entering a room? They adjust themselves, fix their collars, rub their hair and some of them will even stand up in hopes that she will shift her eyes his way for a moment so he can offer her some assistance. The man that is lucky enough to have that beautiful woman often raves about her loveliness, but what do you suppose would happen if that gorgeousness ran out?

I don't understand why today's woman have abandoned their innate ability to love, be loved and affectionate, only to chase material and superficial things. Is it a gross lack of knowledge and understanding or has the older generation failed to implant those values in the new generation?

We often get caught up and entangled in the use of our senses to drive attraction to someone; we completely disregard the philosophical, intellectual, spiritual and psychological stimulation, which are the elements that reach her soul; not the physical.

To love the soul of a black woman you should make it your mission to take out moments each day to connect with her spiritually by giving praise to God because believe me she does. In fact, take out time to do it together, and be sure to thank God for her being in your life.

Understand this, after all difficulties come ease, but God doesn't want you to try to get out of difficulties prematurely; it's the storm that makes you stronger and prepares you for what's to come, but you can't create your own calamities and expect to be bailed out just because you start praying.

That was my biggest problem, creating my own issues and not executing the wisdom and knowledge that I long before possessed, however loving the soul of a black woman is as much understanding as it is applying what you know.

As you read this book the thought may enter your mind that "I" didn't use good and sound judgment when it came to relationships but in order for me to possess the knowledge that I have gain I had to endure some difficulties and most importantly, I'm speaking on what I experienced and am not trying to tell anyone else that lessons will fit you without some adjustments.

The key is to not look for love but to recognize it when it's put in front of you. You cloud your mind, which is your soul, when you're looking for it, and you get caught up most of the time in the physical. God created us of our own free will; as such we choose to endure many of the situations that we go through when it comes to relationships.

Although I knew from the first conversation with my ex that she had anger issues, has been hurt in the past, and suffers from bipolar disorder, I elected of my own free will to continue because I sincerely felt that I could make a difference in her world. I also felt that our paths were meant to cross and I will openly admit that the experience made me so much stronger.

Some of you readers will make the comment, "what does he know? He can't even keep a relationship." Well let me offer you another perspective; I would rather go to war with a man who's been in battle, than to go to battle with a man who has only read or theorized about it. Having-lasting relationship doesn't always mean that you're an expert on what makes relationships work; it could just mean that the two of them were meant to be together and the chemistry is really strong.

I often hear people who have been in five year or longer marriages or relationships speak of the little things, but I can't help but wonder how those people handle or would handle some major problems or a break up. I'm not a love doctor, a relationship expert or psychologist; I'm just a man with way more experience than I cared to gain in my life-time, but I am grateful that I have finally come to a place in life where I can now apply my wisdom and knowledge to having a healthy and life-long lasting relationship and hopefully marriage.

I am an educated man, though neither one of my degrees is in Psychology or even Sociology; a degree to me is only the reflection of a person's ability to understand and retain academic information. Experience is the hardest teacher and the best lesson plan that you can ever receive.

My experience with my ex motivated me to become more educated on her condition. Each time there was a negative occurrence between us I grew stronger and stronger; my knowledge and understanding became deeper and deeper. My patience was constantly tested and my tolerance burgeoned with every passing moment. I have been asked several times by many people how I sleep at night knowing that she was bipolar?

I could only offer a response that based on my growing knowledge of people with a bipolar disorder they have a certain "air of arrogance," if they have an urge to hurt you, they want you to see it coming, hence they are more prone to attempt to cause you harm while you are awake, alert and focused on them than when you're asleep. Of course, anything can happen and there's no conclusive scientific proof of that.

Bipolar disorder is defined as a lifelong condition that can affect both how you feel and how you act. It is a mood disorder thought to be caused by chemical imbalances in the brain that can result in extreme swings in mood—from manic highs to depressive lows. To be diagnosed with bipolar disorder, you must have experienced a high period (mania).

Bipolar mania is described as an "extreme high," or feeling unusually great. Most people with bipolar disorder when ill or when symptomatic experience more lows than highs. These lows are known as bipolar depression. Bipolar disorder affects approximately 5.7 million American adults, or about 2.6 percent of the U.S. population age 18 and older in a given year. The median age of onset for bipolar disorders is 25 years.

Being the stubborn person that I am, I had to ask myself a question. "Are all bipolar people alone?" My answer was "no," therefore, it became my mission to ignore it and make the relationship work. The problem was I didn't put enough time and effort into the preparation. I was trying to learn as I went along and that just doesn't work in this type of situation.

Life is one of the toughest teachers that you will ever face. I never in a million years anticipated being with a woman with a bipolar disorder, but now stimulated by the valuable lesson I learned from this experience I am armed and prepared to deal with it in the future; not that I want to.

One might feel that any woman in love and is hurt would yield a high degree of anger, hurt and pain, but there's something uniquely different about the black woman. When "any" woman loves, she loves deep and hard, and she's emotionally driven, but the thing that sets the black woman apart is she carries with her the painful memories of how her ancestors were treated by the white man, as such, it is deeply embedded in her that there is an automatic mechanism of refusal to accept anything less than excellence and pure love from the black man.

Sometimes our inconsistency and sudden change causes massive problems. I believe that whatever 2 people do to make each other fall in love they should be held accountable to doing to keep each other in love. I realize that people change physically and sometimes situations may have a major effect on behavior and attitudes, but dealing with adverse situations is a learned behavior and you never know what you know until you know it.

The black society seemingly is terminally plagued with an unwritten, unstudied and unsubstantiated syndrome called the "Angry black woman" syndrome and I never took the time and effort to learn anything about it because as soon as I detected it I was gone! It derived from one of those office place or neighborhood bar conversations riddled with shade-tree philosophy because of the dynamic behavior and verbal comments from a black woman who was pushed into a corner by some man and she came out fighting.

All men in general desire peace with women, but we as black men want our women to be sweet, kind and talk nice to us all the time, but we do so many things to trigger their negative manners and angry speaking towards us. The problem is due to the "follow the leader" mentality society that we live in, the media, social networking and public platforms has caused women to arm themselves with this "bad attitude" for self-protection.

Attitude is defined as an expression of favor or disfavor toward a person, place, thing, or event the (**attitude object**). Prominent psychologist Gordon Allport once described attitudes "the most distinctive and indispensable concept in contemporary social psychology." Attitude can be formed from a person's past and present. Attitude is also measurable and changeable as well as influencing the person's emotion and behavior.

Therefore, left up to mass interpretation I define "bad attitude" as the negative verbal or physical responses from someone, which are stimulated by unfavorable actions, words or behavior from others that are directed towards the accused. I never gave myself the opportunity to deal with a woman with an anger issue or a bad attitude before meeting my ex.

Here's the part of the definition that is not readily accepted, **"which are stimulated by."** I guarantee you that if you diagnose and dig deep enough into every black woman, or any woman's mind for that matter, that we identify as having a bad attitude we will find a source or trigger points that caused the negative expressions. The challenge is getting to the very bottom and determining the primary cause and rudiments. So here are the missing elements, **"patience and aggression."**

Gentlemen, we have to gain the patience to research, learn, accept and embrace the things that motivated our women to feel disrespected, which drives their behavior. Remember, Eve wasn't designed to be ugly and nasty towards Adam; circumstances create feelings, which ignite actions that are interpreted as bad behavior.

Try to consider all circumstances, especially the ones that you generate. Let's take ourselves out of denial. We are 75% responsible for the negative attitudes that women display towards us and I'm being moderate with that percentage.

LESSON # 1, "EMPTY YOUR BUCKET."

Anticipation is perhaps one of the greatest attributes that you can gain and use to solidify your quest to loving the soul of a black woman. Have you ever taken notice of the gigantic smile that drapes a woman's face when you do something for her or give her a gift and she says, "oh my God! It's like you read my mind or something!" Or she might say, "It's not the gift that counts but the thought behind it."

You didn't read her mind; you just observed and listened! Of course there are some things we do naturally that appeal to a woman's inner-self, but it means so much more when there is a reflection of effort on your part.

Ladies, you have so much displaced aggression just dwelling inside of you until it's almost as though you're waiting to encounter someone to unload on. Realize that being aggressive when striving for a goal or accomplishment is okay, but you have to direct that aggression towards men. Spend that energy on digging out and embracing, that's right, I said, "embracing" the root cause of your frustrations. Once you identify those roots pull them up!

Everyone, don't be confused about what we "need." The thing that we seem to antagonistically seek out is of the flesh; your soul is of the mind. If we all condition our minds to intake, process and disseminate aggression, then we can control how we "act" upon our feelings and emotions. I'm sorry people, but I have to tell it like it is!

There is no way in hell that my parents, your parents and all the couples generations before us could have sustained 50 plus years if our Mothers didn't practice this philosophy and our Fathers didn't use this method.

So what about when the black woman goes to the white man? Now that's a horse of a different color; no pun intended. The first thing that the black woman says when she makes the decision to "go to the other side" is that the white man knows how to treat his lady. Why shouldn't he know how to treat you good? He's had enough years of practice on how to treat you bad; that's if Newton's law is actually true… "He takes me places, he buys me things, and he respects me." I can't help but wonder if that respect is genuine or fear.

The black man is driven by pride, while the white man is driven by desire. I remember Woody Harrelson's character in "White Men Can't Jump," saying to Wesley Snipes' character, "You'd *rather* look good and lose than look bad and win… That's a *black man*." A black man would rather "look good" and lose and a white man will "look bad" and win!

That's pride versus desire; the pride of looking good and the desire to succeed. The white man's image is not predicated on how the world views him from the outside but how the world views his impact on society and his accomplishments.

I am a black man that knows how to love a black woman, but never took the time to practice and execute what I know. So what do I mean by that? Keep reading and you will figure it out. It is a very powerful thing but wasted energy to be a great teacher but never give your students a chance to learn. It's even worse, however, to be a great scholar and don't practice what you know. A very close friend of mine said to me, **"It's okay to fall, because falling is not failing. The difference between the two is the "I" and the "L"; as long as you don't let the L**

become an I you can get up, dust yourself off and begin again! " jb brown.

I've been in more marriages and relationships than I care to disclose, but I will as the chapters progress, and I've learned so much from them. The problem, as stated a moment ago, is I didn't apply what I know in my last relationship. It's kind of like confronting a fear; you walk right up to it, stare it down, then walk away, but if you conquer it, then it's defeated and you can put it behind you. That's what happened in my situation.

The lessons learned that I denote in this book, I already knew, but was too damned stubborn to execute them too; I became a victim of progression. I was standing on my foundation, but functioning from someone else's house and that caused me to allow the buggy to come before the horse. I would like to share another spoken-word piece with you as an expression of my desire for a woman.

THE OTHER NIGHT

The other night I felt something move me

Like a do when he's chasing a bone

Her well-kept extensions got a feel of new dimensions

As I proceeded into the delightful zone.

Everything that pleased me doubled

Although my vision was 20/20 clear

The pumps made her humps stand out like the mumps

As twin moans infiltrated my ear

Tritonguelation was brought into existence

And satisfaction rose to a new height

Not a care to despair and we were well aware

Of the pleasure we shared

Jbstar 2004

Each Oyster contains a new pearl that has to be polished to its own dimensions and characteristics. We are not going to like the same things; that's what makes us individuals. You may take a basic approach to loving the soul of a black woman, but the feelings and reactions will vary, therefore the recipe has to be tailored to fit each appetite. Sometimes I wish I could go back to the old days.

A guy sees a girl he likes and simply composed a note; "I love you, do you love me? Yes or No; Circle one." If she circled "yes," it's on! The romance began with the two of them meeting at her locker between classes, and then came the exchange of phone numbers and personal items such as his letterman's jacket, class ring or a heart shaped necklace.

That action established the connection. Of course they ate lunch together from that point forward closely followed by a definitive display of affection shown by the undivided attention rewarded to each during recess. The most expedient way back then to let everyone know about the newly developed love affair was to intentionally show up late at a home football or basketball game so they can walk in together, thereby diverting everyone's attention towards them.

Folks in the stands would try to inconspicuously lean over and whisper something about the couple. Of course now we have texting, so it can actually be done inconspicuously, then later at the precise time they "sneak" away to kiss under the bleachers. At that time in the union things had sustained the basic tests of long nights on the phone asking each other "what are you doing and what do you want to talk about?"

Therefore, it was time to go to McDonald's, which in those days was only one step away from the tip of the iceberg! In those days you were really official when you went to Red Lobster. Sadly, today going to Red Lobster is like going to McDonald's and as for the class ring or letterman's jacket, many women expect the man to pay her rent or take on some bills the first week they meet. God I miss the old days!

One of the most beautiful things about the old days and young love was everything was fresh and new. Today we bring too many "old" lies into our "new" relationships. I never in my life thought I would see a day as it is now where women are such liars! In the old days when a guy asked a girl for her number, if she liked him, she would give it to him to call. If she didn't, then he just wouldn't get the number. Today a lying female will look right in your face, take out her cell phone, put your number in and never call, instead of just telling the guy that she's not interested. Yet, in the same breath women have the nerve to say that men don't respect them.

How can you expect men to honor you if you don't honor yourself? Lying is a learned behavior and the more you do it the more comfortable it becomes. It carries over into everything that you do. One of the most peaceful feelings that I have ever experienced is honesty. I'm going to share with you in chapter 10 one of the worst lies that I have ever lived. I thank God for seeing me through what could have yielded the most catastrophic outcome of my life; I could have been writing this book from prison.

Right now, let me share with you a little white lie I told that turned into a black cat. I was at Wal-Mart in the health and beauty aid section when I noticed a very pretty lady walk by. Immediately, my entire focus shifted towards her as she made her way to the pet food aisle. Hesitantly, I made my approach, as to ensure that a jealous male was not lurking closely behind. She stopped at the cat food and I surreptitiously walked right beside her and pretended to be interested in cat food as well. "Hello." I politely rendered a greeting and she responded with equal kindness. "Hi."

"Wal-Mart sure is proud of their cat food, are they?" I said, as I attempted to make small talk. "I know, right! You have a cat?" Bam! There it was; the perfect intro, followed closely by the perfect "little white lie." "Yep!" I said, excitedly, and then closed the gap between us. "Oh, me too!" She shared. "What's your cat's name?" I asked, knowing that I was the least bit interested in her damn cat. "Peebles!" She said, as the smile on her face grew more and more friendly. "What's your cat's name?" She asked. "Mr. Peeps!" I continued to lie through my teeth.

"Maybe Pebbles and Mr. Peeps can get together and play sometimes; Mr. Peeps might be her new boyfriend." I said confidently, although I was really talking about myself in reference to her. "I don't think so!" She quickly replied,

"Pebbles is a male too. I named him Pebbles because I thought he was a girl when I first got him, then when I took him for a checkup, the Vet said he was a male, so I just kept the name." "Oh, well I don't think Mr. Peeps is gay, so I guess there won't be any romance there!"

We both laughed, and then I knew I had gained valuable ground. "I'm Jerome," and extended my hand for a more formal introduction. "I'm Teresa!" She replied. "I realize that you don't know me from a can of cat food, but I would love to have dinner with you tonight, if you're not busy and there's not a "Mr. Teresa." I said, jokingly.

"I would love to; I don't have any plans and no, there's no "Mr. Teresa!" I'm single." She told me as I began to feel a tingling sensation. "Jackpot!" I thought, while leaving out one very important detail. "I didn't actually have a cat!" She used her phone to call mine to give me her number and off our separate ways we went to prepare for a night of romance! We agreed to meet at Red Lobster, although I would have gladly picked her up to show how much of a gentleman I was.

To keep up the lie, I bought $10.00 worth of cat food, spent 3 hours hunting down shelters to find a cat, a cage and a bunch of damned toys that just cluttered up my apartment. I went on the internet and read about cats as much as I could, and are you ready for this? We went on four dates and she vamped!

It was a done deal and I was stuck with that freaking cat, running, jumping, climbing, pissing and shitting all over my apartment! My sister often teases me about that, asking every time I meet a new female, if I went out and bought a snake, rabbit, hamster or some other flea-bitten rodent.

Being honest comes across as nonchalant and non-caring at first, but the after effects are awesome. Some people may even view it as rudeness or being an ass, but understand that we weren't put on this earth to like or be liked by everybody. The key is to be true to yourself and the immediate people that mean the most to you.

My ex has claimed to have been raped by 11 guys before me; I was the 12th claim! Don't worry, I explain in chapter 10. Please don't misunderstand me, rape does happen and I'm completely appalled at the mere thought of it!

I lose all sense of morality just thinking about a man even hitting a woman. I have family members that were victims of spousal and boyfriend abuse; If it wasn't for my brother and nephew tackling me in response to someone hitting one of my sisters years ago, I would have probably gone to prison back then because I had blood in my eyes, and there was no doubt that I would have killed him or beat him to within inches of his life being over, and I've never regretted that feeling.

In the old days unless someone was a hell raiser in elementary school or just a congenital liar there was just nothing to lie about. As I mentioned about texting, technology also plays a major role in today's life-style. Children are practically born with an IPad or cell phone in their hands but everything in society now is so rushed that no one wants to take time to date, which is a process within itself.

Dating and relationships take time and patience, which is why they don't last in present times. It is an ongoing process; my parents were married for 49 years before my Father died and I have two friends whose parents have sustained the same longevity. My best friend is currently approaching his 25th anniversary and I envy them every day.

I really hate being single and now I finally realize and accept that I'm to blame. Although Monee' suffers from anger management and Bi-polar disorder, I should have taken time to research, study and understand the conditions and therefore taken steps to put things in place, including my behavior, to prevent the destruction of our relationship.

Before you can love the soul of a black woman you must first get to know her soul. To love the soul is to love her mind, which produces the thoughts that generate and control her actions. Therefore, to accept her actions is to understand her thoughts, hence embracing her mind, which clears the pathway to loving her soul.

This is not a "one size fits all" situation. Each person must set and follow her own standards. Once you do, stick to them. I need you to understand that everyone doesn't match everyone. Opposing traits trigger bad chemistry; once two people find each other with matching characteristics then love each other through those traits and embellish those qualities.

When two people accept each other their attributes are not always gauged as good or bad. Gentlemen, if she's a smoker and you don't mind, then you should know through her actions that part of her daily thoughts will be to smoke a cigarette; therefore part of your mission of loving her soul would be to buy her a pack and flick her bic sometimes.

It's really a simple concept; just remember that all actions are preceded by a thought. You can believe it if you want to when someone says, "I just reacted; I didn't think about it." What they really mean is they didn't think it through.

People are always making excuses that they do things without thinking, they were drunk or angry.

That's some bull! People do things without thinking it through; there's nothing new under the sun. As for being drunk or angry, that's when things are said and done that subconsciously they don't have the guts to do otherwise. Once again I'm speaking of someone's actions.

The loving black woman goes to great lengths to please her man. You sometimes feel that you are up against every other single element in the world, but most of the time you are just competing with yourself and your man. Ask yourself a question, ladies, have you ever thought or said to someone else, "I do everything for him; I want to know what it feels like to be pampered sometimes?"

Gentlemen, don't think that "only" rubbing her feet every now and then is enough; it's not even close and please don't believe that spending money buying expensive gifts is the answer. Sometimes it's as simple as sacrificing 10 minutes of the game by muting or turning off the TV and listening to her tell you about her day. Try it!

Discussion question—What should be the maximum number of differences allowed before rejecting a relationship?

CHAPTER II

"BUGGY BEFORE THE HORSE"

In some places people use the horse and buggy for transportation or entertainment and the way it is driven is by dangling a carrot in front of the horse's face. He attempts to eat the carrot while stepping towards it, thereby pulling the buggy. Of course he doesn't realize that every time he steps, the carrot moves forward too and maintains the same distance, so he always thinks he can reach it.

Shutters are affixed to the sides of the horse's head which are controlled and moved from side to side, which determines the direction the horse travels. A slight pull backwards against the reign and closing of the shutters over the horse's eyes brings the whole thing to a halt.

A few years ago I decided that what I was doing as far as my relationships, including the type of women I was choosing, was not working. Therefore, after a very thorough cleansing of my life, I set some standards for myself and the lady that would become my wife, best friend and life-long confidant.

I playfully considered that woman to be my "carrot," so I developed a list of categories that women I meet would fall into based on where they fell according to my list of qualifications. There are three levels; from top to bottom there is the carrot, the boo and the cuddle-bunny.

To be my carrot she must possess the following characteristics. She cannot smoke cigars, cigarettes or marijuana, no illegal drugs; I am 47 years old and my children raring days are over as my own children are both grown, therefore I prefer she doesn't have small children, no mental health conditions such as anger management issues, Bi-polar disorder or epilepsy, only social drinking, no compelling desire to hang out in bars, she must enjoy going to family gatherings, both hers and mine.

We must attend the same church, no outside personal male friends or ongoing friendship with an ex, no sleeping in separate rooms, no attending parties or gatherings without each other, must take my last name in marriage and she must love to kiss. Hell of a list, huh? Well that's what it's gonna take to be my carrot and I'm not backing down from it.

Now please understand that having this list doesn't make me a bad guy no more than it makes a woman that doesn't live up to it a bad girl; it only means that we are not the right choice for each other.

The second category is a boo; there are two levels in this stage. The first class boo and the entry level boo. Let's begin with the 1st class Boo; she has most of the characteristics of a carrot but the missing traits are correctable. For example if she smokes, she can stop that but if she does drugs, smokes marijuana, has anger management issues and a bad attitude, then she's automatically disqualified. At this level she can spend the night with me and perhaps leave a tooth-brush and a change of clothes, she can answer the door and perhaps even my phone, and she can meet co-workers and associates but not close personal friends or the family.

The entry level boo possesses more than half of the qualities to become a carrot but the key is she has to have a clear understanding of what it takes to be my carrot and a strong willingness to work on herself to meet the qualifications. She can spend the night but must leave the next morning, she can leave a tooth-brush, but no change of clothes; she can't answer the door or my phone and we can be seen together in public but can't meet any close personal friends or co-workers.

Category 3 is a cuddle-bunny; this is a basic "cut-buddy." She doesn't have any of the qualities to become a carrot; she can't be seen with me in public, she can't spend the night, she get no special privileges and it's basically all about the sex. As I take you through this journey you're going to find that I broke all my rules. I basically took a cuddle-bunny and tried to make her into a carrot. The sad part is my best friend sensed it the first time he met her and I knew it within the first month that we were together but I would not walk away.

August 29th 2012, 2:35, midday afternoon; the sky was clear, my mind was open and my heart fluttered in anticipation of our first encounter. She emerged from the sidewalk and glided gracefully into the small, yet eloquent restaurant located just across from the train station on Main Street. The place was empty, which was perfect for me because that meant fewer distractions.

Her painted on, purple tights affectionately hugged every voluptuous curve of her well-toned lower half, as it made me wish to had been reincarnated as fiber so "I" could have the euphoric pleasure of being woven into the design that embraced her Gluteus Maximus (ass) all day long. Her preferred reference name is simply, Monee'.

Though she only stood 5' 3" tall in the natural state, the 6" heels combined with her 3" box haircut raised her to an astonishing 6 feet. Of course, being that I'm only 5' 7" she towered over me, hence leaving me with the pleasure of knowing that "horizontally," we would match to a "T!" Her upper torso was precisely proportioned and matched naturally with the bottom half.

She had the most perfect jawline that I had ever seen. Her facial contour was so well-defined that it left me struggling with deciding which set of "cheeks" I wanted to kiss the most; I was confident that eventually, I would possess the privilege of kissing them both.

Encircled by slightly slanted lids, her eyes shined like marbles that glistened from the sunlight; it took me back to my days in grade-school on the playground when I cherished those little shiny round jewels so much that I never dared to "put them in the pot" to be clanked against by some other chipped up player only to be taken away from me in the heat of battle. She smiled as we greeted, which granted me the opportunity to witness first-hand and up close the beautifully designed structure of her unflawed teeth.

I remember thinking at that moment, "Oh my God! What did I do to deserve this?" Then the entire experience intensified when she spoke; such confidence, such eloquence, such grace. I could feel my penis beginning to rise and harden just from the mere sound of her voice. That's when I knew, undoubtedly, "this is gonna be mine."

As we sat there going through the formalities of eating and making casual conversation to "get to know each other," her brown, 129 pound, athletically shaped frame kept crying out to me, "take me!" and my 171 pound nicely toned body was screaming right back at her, "I'm gonna pound you like it's my first and last piece of coochie combined!"

I was careful to conceal my lust for her with a smile that she quickly grew fond of and would eventually fall in love with. I could sense by her uncontrolled squirming and constant giggle that moisture had infiltrated her inner thighs and she would soon make an excuse to go to the bathroom so she could gently remove the wetness with a wad of tissue.

The aroma of her juices was so potent that even the smell emanating from the kitchen of the restaurant was unable to drown it out. Physically, she was everything a man could want in a woman and at "that" moment I could see nothing else; at that moment, I wanted to see "nothing" else.

She would progress twice more to the bathroom to give care to the persistent surge of her sexual stream of nectar. The more she flowed, the more I wanted to taste her. The conversation continued and I went "old school" by offering her a note that read, "I love you. Do you love me? Yes or No? Circle one."

I was so mesmerized by her sensuality and we were both so hypnotized by the physical attraction that we ignored the personality traits that would later cause us not to stay together. We talked, laughed, shared food and practically fell in love, or "at least in lust," in that little restaurant. She described her profession to me and intrigue caused my thoughts to briefly deviate as I listened intensely.

Although by this time, I was so captivated by her smile and infatuated with her voice, that all I could truly focus on was how bad I wanted to taste her tongue and feel my rock-hard penis inside her as I simultaneously lick and suck her nipples until she screamed out my name.

She was an artist in the most natural sense. She created designs from the biological strains that emerged from the roots of the most superior region of the human body. (She braids hair) I was fascinated to say the least and quickly accepted her invitation to personally witness this artistry. We left the restaurant, of which the tab I paid, and departed the area together with my vehicle left behind. We were still so distracted by each other's presence that a pedestrian nearly paid the price of a one on one collision with the SUV that we were traveling in. I thank God that her attention was redirected quickly enough to avoid disaster.

We were shortly joined by her youngest of 4 offspring then proceeded to her place of business. The more I sat patiently watching her "do her thing," the more turned on we both became and it was just a matter of time before the sweat of our anatomies would blend like the stirring of cream into a hot cup of coffee.

That was the first time in over 40 years of life and nearly 30 years of sex that I "came" on myself from just watching her move around. I recall the self-contained excitement I yielded when she took off her high-heel shoes, but her ass and calves remained just as defined and unaffected as if she was still wearing them.

"Shit! Damn, she's fine!" The fantasies just continued to stomp out any other thoughts that even attempted to enter my mind at the time. "Don't get me wrong, I'm not some sex fiend with pretentious thoughts of sexual hunger." "I do value other traits in women." Shamefully, I hadn't made love to a woman in several months and though I was honestly hung up between deciding if I wanted to have sex with her, make love to her or just bang the hell out of her.

It is important that it's understood that black women have peculiarities which sets them apart from any other race on the planet. Just continue to read and you will see what I mean... Let me share another piece with you.

DAMN SHE'S FINE

The aroma of the wine triggers thoughts in my mind

Like the moisture of an oyster as our bodies intertwine

Bringing love, bringing peace, even moments of despair

Tantalizing tender memories of her body laying bare

Nipples gleaming; constant dreaming of the taste that's so divine

Giving meaning to the feeling of the rhythm; damn she's fine!

jbstar 06

See, we live in a "follow the leader" society and as such, one of the astigmatisms that became an epidemic of great proportions through recent years was the "Angry black woman" syndrome. Unfortunately, this caused the black man to approach his female opposite with a predetermined mindset that they are all mad at the world because of what some other brother has done to them; by my own admission, I'm guilty of the same. In a previous conversation with her on the phone I accused her of being plagued with the syndrome. Of course, she denied it and made every effort to prove otherwise. I must admit she was extremely convincing in that attempt.

We spent several hours at her establishment and I endured one of the most out of body experiences that I had ever been blessed with. By this time I had already made love to her just from watching her grace the room with her movement, and then I was ready to explode. She wrapped up business for the day, closed down the shop and we proceeded to her residence to settle in with her children. After her domestic duties were complete we returned to Main Street to retrieve my vehicle, then off to McDonald's we went!

She insisted on treating me for dessert and I reluctantly but humbly obliged. We had ice cream sundaes, we talked some more, I showed her a card magic trick and we indulged our first embrace, which became the precursor for our first kiss outside in the parking lot as I made my move while opening the passenger door for her.

Our tongues intertwined like the ribbons of a twirler in an Olympic competition. We unselfishly exchanged saliva as the soft smacking sound of our lips provided confirmation of our ultimate and untamed attraction. I offered to take her to my apartment, and with her acceptance opened a pathway to ecstasy that could never be reversed.

Upon arrival, there was very little much else to "talk" about, at least at that time. We stretched out on my small but adequately sized sofa and picked up where we left off with our kissing. **"Reader's discretion is advised!"** Slowly, I began to remove articles of clothing from her body and she returned the gestures in-kind. I started with only her shirt, as not to seem like I was rushing the situation. I gently pulled her "B" size bra cup aside to gain access to her hardened nipples and proceeded to softly lick and nibble my way around her areolas. She moaned quietly and her aggression attempted to expedite the process was consistently halted by my carefully thought out plan to "take my time with her."

I wanted to "do her" softly, gradually and tenderly. I wanted her to know it was me inside and remember that I had been there. I wanted there to be absolutely no doubt as to whether or not she wanted to do it again and again and again. After several prolonged moments of alternating my kisses between her lips and her nipples I finally removed her bra completely, and then unhurriedly ventured my way down to her waist line.

"Oooh! Oh, Baby!" she said repeatedly as I continued to have my way with her. I tickled her pantie-line and fondled her clitoris as it stood at attention in comparison to the blood-filled, stiffened flesh that dwelled "impatiently" between my legs.

I decisively surrendered to passion, peeled off her last stitch of clothing, picked her up and carried her to my bed, then unselfishly inserted my erection as deep inside her as my scrotum would allow. I still reflect upon the thought of wishing I could put my entire self inside her. I had suspended contemplation of wanting to be a baby again and just crawl right back inside, except, this time around the womb that bared me would not be that of my Mother. The more she expressed how much she loved it, the more force I exerted with each thump…

I thrusted her harder and deeper than any vagina that I had ever explored in life. It felt like the perfect fit and she confirmed my suspicions with numerous outcries of emotion. "Oh God! Damn I love your dick inside of me!" She called out, as her hands gripped my ass, pulling me to maximum capacity with each stroke, then vigorously rubbing my biceps while they flexed in support of holding my body in the push-up position. "Baby, baby, baby," she continued, as I experienced brief moments of feeling like I was in a TLC video being slapped on my ass by "Left-Eye." "Yeah, girl, I got so much love for you!"

This unrestricted action went on for hours! "That's right, I said hours." With each ounce of my flesh that submerged inside her canal caused my body to shiver and shake like the leaves of a Florida palm tree trying to withstand the dangerously high winds of a tropical storm. All that seemed to matter at the time was the feeling that I got from gripping her ass, rubbing her titts, licking her nipples, kissing her lips, sucking her tongue and banging that coochie like she was the last female on earth and I was the last man.

I had my share of sexual escapades and some of them yielded results that weren't exactly pleasing to both parties involved, but for the first time ever, it didn't seem to matter what I did or how I did it she was pleased. She didn't push me back, nor squeeze her legs together to reduce the pressure from my aggression. She didn't scoot back or try to create a shock absorber in any way.

Her weakness, as she very subtly revealed to me, was the back of her neck and her knees being kissed. You know this only increased my motivation to go straight to these points of interest. Every time I put her knees up by her head and simultaneously licked them as I pushed firmer and firmer she responded with, "Oh Baby, I'm flowing all over your d**k!" She was so wet I felt like I was dropping my shaft in a glass of water.

My eyes rolled back in my head, my toes pointed, the volcano erupted and hot lava spewed so forcefully it could have pressure washed an old house. I could see no evil and in case you haven't done the math or are questioning it; yes, this was the first night...

The subsequent nights were filled with equal passion and desire. We humped every chance we got and it didn't matter where we were. One night she took me to a little pizza joint where she hung out sometimes and she was wearing a short black dress. That was when I confirmed that she didn't wear panties and she used tampons to contain her continuous flow of juices because she was in her sexual peak at 34 years old. After a light dinner of pizza and dialogue we indulged in dessert outside in my truck in the form of "butt-naked," body-bumping rage.

I sat in my passenger seat and she climbed on top of me and rode me as if she was competing for 1st prize on a mechanical bull in a crowded nightclub and could give a fat baby's ass about who was watching. Our bodies intertwined like the strands of a Twisler stick. I damn near felt sorry for the poor white man sitting in his car next to us.

I'm sure he got on his phone and told his wife, "honey, can you believe there's two niggers in a truck parked next to me having sex!?" The truck was rocking, the windows were fogged up and people were walking by like nothing was out of the ordinary. The sad part about it was that we still didn't recognize that we had put the **"Buggy Before The Horse."**

What the hell does he mean by that, you're probably wondering? Well, let me simplify it for you. Perhaps you need to go back to the beginning and see if you can find the part where I said that we actually took the time to get to know each other. We didn't! We were so blinded by our sexual attraction that we never realized that nearly every time we attempted to just "talk" it turned into an argument.

I became so confused that whenever it even hinted like we were going to argue I would just start hugging and kissing her, then before we knew it we were having sex. She constantly told me that I had the best penis that she ever had and I constantly used it to my advantage.

From the first day we met I said to her that I only had two requirements of my lady in a relationship, "be nice to me and keep me sexually satisfied." She taught me many valuable lessons throughout our 14 months together, "never to make that statement again was one of those lessons."

LESSON 2, "DON'T MAKE UNFOUNDED STATEMENTS."

She taught me that I devalued myself as a man by saying that because the black woman has so much more to offer and by saying that she only have to be nice and satisfy me sexually not only relinquishes her of her Godly duties as a woman, but gives her an excuse to be far less than what she was put here to be and has the ability to do.

Furthermore, from the male perspective I deprive myself of what Proverbs say a virtuous woman should be. God didn't intend for women to compete with men. However God created us of our own free will and because of that "follow the leader" mentality that I mentioned earlier more and more women are doing just that. They are working outside the home, becoming doctors, lawyers and even Pastors in some cases.

Now I acknowledge that this may be a bit touchy but women were not meant to be Pastors. There are women in construction, policemen and even running for the Presidency. Don't misunderstand me, I do believe that women have their place in society, but I also agree that if a man is to support that idea, then he must be ready, willing and able to provide for it. My problem was that I could not provide for it…

If Monee' had her way, she would be at home wearing nothing more than a sheet every day waiting for me to come in so she could ask me, "How do you want it?" See, that was another lesson. We can't classify all women the same or all people period. In a conversation with a lady from my past, she made the statement that "there is no such thing as a sole-mate and I don't think that there's any one man for me." I disagreed.

Of course this sparked an intense debate, which was alright with me because I think I'm pretty good at debating. I allowed her to present her case and make her points and in return I led off with one simple question. "Do you know what DNA is?" She embarrassed herself with a feeble attempt to respond intelligently, but ignorance prevailed and she became somewhat submissive.

Only to show off my knowledge, I then said "it stands for Deoxyribonucleic Acid. It's the largest molecule in the human body that defines who we are as individuals." Impressed by my intellectual response she became somewhat aroused, and continued to listen. "There are over 7 billion people in the world, 1.5% of which are twins. Now, each of us have two eyes, ears, nose, a mouth with teeth, cheekbones, hairlines, eyebrows, eyelashes and even eyeballs and yet, except for the twins, we all look different."

My next question was, "Do you believe in God?" "Yes, of course," she emphatically replied. "Do you believe as it says in Romans 28 that God created the universe and all that's within it?" I followed up. "Yes..." she continued. I then replied, "So if God created 7 billion people all to look different through DNA, then what makes you believe that he can't create just one person for you?" "Wow," she said with a slight look of discernment. "No one has ever broken it down to me like that before. I guess it is possible." "You just have to find him. No one said that would be easy." I said with a slight gloat. What's my point? I ask you.

People are not the same, but it doesn't mean that just because someone is not right for "you" that it makes them a bad person. It doesn't make you any better than that person or that person any better than you. When you take the time to learn who a black woman is, you give yourself the opportunity to enhance who you are.

What I interpreted for so long as "attitude" is really passion and desire. She speaks with such conviction that it's almost scary; not because of fear, but because of reality. She is equally as obsessive about right as she is about wrong. It's sad that I never really took the time to take possession of the gifts in her that God put right in front of me.

Newton's third law says that **"every action has an equal and opposite reaction."** However, just knowing this quote doesn't mean a thing if you don't know what it means. She used to say to me all the time, **"you are so selfish,"** and Karma is a bitch, but did I hear her? No, because I had already fooled myself that dishing good tube-steak would resolve any and all ill feelings that she came up with.

I fooled myself to believe that showing up at her home or business, unannounced, with candy, balloons or a card somehow dispensed the illusion that I wasn't selfish but the selfish act was the entire reaction was based on how "I" felt about doing it, instead of how "she" felt about it being done.

I enjoyed listening to her tell me how nice something looked that I created and listening to her brag to her friends or clients about what she got from me. Instead, the focus should have been on how good she's feeling at the time of reception and what residual feelings she has for the rest of the day. There were times when I would show up at her house, tools in hand, work-clothes on and ready to "fix" something. She only had to mention that something was wrong or broken and there I was to correct it and then spring some good sex on her to cap it off.

I never took the time or spent the effort to understand that what she really wanted was for me to put that same energy into her and let the repair guys do all the handy work. I guess that's how we end up losing our women to the "maintenance man;" while we're busy doing their work, they're busy working it out with our ladies. I would always be so proud after completing a task, but she would always seem happier when I just sat and held her. Unfortunately, I was too blind and stupid to realize that.

A "pet peeve" is a minor annoyance that an individual identifies more as particularly annoying to them, to a greater degree than others may find it. Monee' constantly told me the things she didn't like; verbally, emotionally, physically and spiritually, but my tough outer shell always seemed to suppress my ability to comprehend.

Ladies, unfortunately every man is not going to just be exactly what you want. Sometimes we have to be shaped and molded into your preferred likeness. It is easy for a woman to say, "I'm a lady, so treat me like one," but there is a big difference between a female who looks like a lady, but she "acts" like a man.

No man wants to be spoken to as mean, harsh and nasty by a woman; hell, we don't even want to be spoken to that way by a man! And if you curse worse than a sailor, then how do you expect men to view you with his third eye when he can't get past the surface? There are many things that are not "lady-like" that women have a bad habit of doing on a consistent basis that they have become so comfortable with, it appears natural. Example, watching football, drinking beer, yelling competitively with the others at the TV screen and sitting with her legs gaped wide open in a room full of men.

Am I saying that women shouldn't watch football? Of course not! I'm also not saying that you have to fix the sandwiches and serve up the beverages. However, just because you're in a room full of men doesn't mean you have to become one. So what is "lady-like?" For me, in that situation it would be first and far-most, keep your legs crossed or at least closed. Scream and cheer when something exciting happens or a team scores, but sound like a female, don't deepen your voice to match the tone of a man and grab your crotch when doing so.

Lastly, speak like a lady; don't let every other word that comes out of your mouth be, "Man, shit! You know what I'm saying!" And when it's over, leave! Don't try to sit around and match wits with the guys to show that your balls are just as big as theirs.

What are some things that are lady-like or should be done for you as a lady? Here are some common occurrences that lead to big problems. Let's start with the ladies; don't speak loudly or curse at your man, don't correct a man in public, don't interrupt a man when he's speaking, don't act like you're his Mother, don't nag a man and don't manipulate your man.

Allow your man to learn to open doors for you. Believe it or not, chivalry is a learned behavior. Don't just think a man is going to do these things for you just because you look good. If his Daddy didn't teach him, it may be up to you. Movies work too!

Let him know that you know nothing about changing oil and have no yearning to, smooth your dress out behind you when you're about to sit down, extend your hand when going up or coming down stairs with no rail or getting out of a vehicle, minimize your slang and curse words; especially in public, refrain from calling him foul and ugly names just because you're mad or you disagree about something, and constantly reassure him that you know he's not perfect, but you're only asking him to give you love that's pleasing to you; not the rest of the world.

Ladies, you have to accept the fact that you bring a lot of things on yourself by abandoning the basics to try to hurt or get at him, and when you do, it takes you out of your element as a lady. And ladies, probably one of the most powerful things that you can portray as a lady is stop that BS where you say or imply that if he doesn't do something, then some other man will! Remember ladies, if you want a man to love your soul, then you have to establish the image and remain true to who you are! Don't put beer in a Champagne bottle and expect to not see bubbles and foam.

Now let's talk to the fella's. The man opening doors for a lady, both entering and exiting a vehicle, standing to acknowledge her presence when she walks into the room, ensuring that her car is in good working order, ordering for her at a restaurant when the server is male and vice versa, not being distracted by other women walking by, looking at her when you're talking to her or she's talking to you, not interrupting your conversation by taking a call or responding to a text, not flirting in front of each other, not putting others before her; this especially includes your grown children, not excluding her on major decisions, not forgetting or acknowledging important dates, (to her) and not spending time with female friends or too much time with male friends.

DISCUSSION QUESTION—HOW LONG SHOULD A COUPLE WAIT TO HAVE SEX?

CHAPTER III

"GOTTA LEARN TO LISTEN"

Some of you may find this hard to believe but I have news for you; a person will tell you how to love them if you just learn to listen. Gentlemen, I am really talking to you but Ladies just because you represent a smaller percentage doesn't mean that you're not being watched as well. Ladies and Gentlemen there is power in a compliment and we all have to learn to use it to our advantage. We can't read minds! You would be amazed at how much psychology is involved in relationships.

Something must have attracted you to each other; hold on to whatever it was and exploit it every chance you get. A person loves to gloat, stand up tall and be proud of things they feel good about. I have seen some of the ugliest women step into a crowded room with such a high degree of confidence that she commands attention from everyone there, including you and your man.

"LESSON 3, "KNOW WHAT YOU'RE DEALING WITH."

You gotta let them know! Ladies, if you like a man who is clean shaven, hair tight, smelling good and well dressed, then tell him that! Don't try to get through to your man by complimenting some other guy. Do you realize how stupid that is? All you're gonna do is piss him off and open the door for him to start noticing and complimenting other women in front of you, then your relationship turns into a constant battle between the two of you trying to see who can outdo the other. Let's face it, you don't get into a relationship to compete with each other!

If your man tells you that he likes the way you look in your panties, then get rid of everyone else in the house and walk around in the sexiest pair you have. It's simple, and if he says that he likes the way you look in a certain outfit, that doesn't mean that you have to wear it every other day; just go out and buy some others like it, even if it's at his expense or your sacrifice.

Ladies, I can't tell you how important it is to listen to the man. Most men won't open up because of pride anyway, then that's compounded by nagging, and when you throw berating and emasculation on top of that, it is a recipe for disaster, then you are really tearing your man down and most men won't stand for it. Don't tell your man that men aren't supposed to go on and on about his day! A man's home is his safe haven and you are his confidant. One way or another he's gonna get it out.

No man is going to just keep everything bottled up inside forever, therefore it's equally as important for you to listen to him as it is for him to listen to you; maybe even more so because there's so much more pressure on men. Wait a minute, ladies! Put that thought on hold! You put extra pressure on yourselves. You choose to compete in the world with men. Life was not designed for women to be the head of the household, but I'm gonna refer you back to your bible to expand on that.

There are two phases with seven words each that you should never say to your mate and ladies you are the number one guilty party for saying it. **"What you won't do, someone else will." And "You do you and I'll do me."** That doesn't give you an advantage! It causes unrecoverable damage and it hurts. The black woman puts so much into loving and you have so much power at your disposal.

You just have to learn to control how you act upon your emotions. Notice I said how you "act." We can't control our emotions; they're gonna come no matter what and they are such a beautiful thing.

Learning to love the soul of a black woman is like job announcing, hunting, interviewing, securing and keeping it all rolled up into one life-long procedure. Let me break it down to you. First comes the need to fill the position, closely followed by a job description. Hello! This begins with you! This may sound very much out of the ordinary but you have to create an operator's manual for yourself. I know it may sound funny but I'm for real. You have to format it, write it and enforce it. No one knows you better than you know yourself and trust me, there is no "one size fit all" manual.

Each one is tailored to suit the individual. In this description you state what it is you want and don't cut corners. This is where you are 100% real and true to yourself; then comes the posting. Of course, you're not going to put up an ad or walk around with a shirt that reads, "Hey, I'm available and looking!" Or would you?

Anyway, there are ways that we let others know we are available. Now comes the application process. When a man applies for the position of having your heart you have to scrutinize him very harshly and if he doesn't meet the minimum qualifications, then don't even advance to phase 2 of interviewing; lunch, dinner, or extended conversation.

I'm sorry ladies, and gentlemen too but, "I've got some things working" just don't cut it! During the interview process it is okay to chit-chat about sports and his impending dreams, but the focus should remain on priorities, IE family, friends and affection. To begin with, what's the outlook on family? Here's what needs to be understood; even if there are no children in the picture, the two of you are still a family, whether it's due to the kids being grown and gone or if you both just never decided to have children.

If family doesn't come first behind God, then that's a major conflict and blockage from loving the soul of a black woman. In chapter VII we talk more about outside forces, but for now you need to know that for basic needs you are each other's sole provider.

There is an old movie entitled, "Indecent Proposal," starring Robert Redford, Woody Harrelson and Demi Moore. After viewing it years ago my then mate asked me what I would say if someone offered me a million dollars to have sex with her for just one night to which I replied, "I would say no." She said, "What difference does it make?

You have my heart and my soul belongs to God. My body is just a vessel; it's just sex and wouldn't mean anything, but you would be rich." I simply replied, "God created us of our own free will and though you feel he owns your soul, he actually owns your spirit; you have the freedom to give your body to anyone you choose and you chose me."

To love the soul of a black woman money can't even be a factor. *"Once you learn how to make love to a black woman without touching her you are delving into the deepest depths of her soul. Have you ever experienced or heard of someone just start crying right in the middle of sex? I have... And when asked what's wrong, the answer was simply "I just love you so much!" That's when you know you're making love to her soul and no amount of physical penetration can ever compare to that."* jb brown. Ladies, in laying the groundwork for having your man love your soul you have to prepare every aspect of yourself first.

I saw a lady in the laundry mat one day and I was very attracted to her, so I scanned her hand for a ring, watched her for a few moments to ensure a man wasn't there with her and monitored her clothing to see if I could spot male items. Everything was clear, so I walked over and introduced myself. After saying "Hi" and disclosing her name she said that she was married. I asked, "Why aren't you wearing your ring?" She replied, "I'm allergic to jewelry, so I don't wear it; besides it's really no big deal;

I know, I'm married." I said, "BS!" then I continued, "people have food allergies, and are lactose intolerant but there are food substitutes that people intake every day, so if man can design something that's safe enough to go inside your body, then why is something that you wear on the outside of your body so dangerous?" She couldn't answer and simply said, "Damn! I guess you're right. No one ever put it to me like that before."

Congratulations! You have the position. Now the probationary period starts. This is where the relationship begins but certain benefits are withheld; the amount and which ones are totally up to you. Of course this goes both ways. Ask plenty of questions! Review the background and even the credit history. I speak more in a later chapter regarding Mya Angelou's quote in a later chapter regarding people showing you who they are. During this period you are both exhibiting an enormous amount of patience and observation, and remember that body language speaks much louder than any words you can formulate.

Don't get it twisted, I'm not saying that sex has to be one of those benefits, but women are emotionally driven and sex is directly tied to emotions because it is the most intimate and personal possession that she has to give. Go places together, do things, monitor each other's mannerisms and the way they handle adverse situations. Meet and spend time with family and friends. Assess the work environment if possible and most of all, talk, talk, talk!

Okay, though it may have seemed long you made it through the probationary period. It's time to celebrate however; you still must proceed with caution and execute ongoing assessments. What was done to get each other must be done to keep each other. You can't just stop! You can't just start doing things differently. This is that "power in a compliment" I spoke of; it makes you feel so appreciated, but please remember those 7 words not to say.

Here are some things that should never be asked for. A woman should never have to ask for the trash to be taken out, doors to be opened, chairs to be pulled out, heavy objects lifted or moved, yard work done, her vehicle being maintenance, for her to put first, a good morning, good-bye or good-night kiss, household items fixed, to take her out, to accompany her at outings or important events and including her in important decisions.

Wait a minute Ladies, you have to groom yourself first! As a black man, or any man for that matter, who wants to love the soul of a black woman he too should never ask for certain things. This includes, but not limited to his food to be prepared and given to him, sex to be available and willing for him, support him in his endeavors, stand behind his decisions, and compliment him.

The majority of my mistakes were truly innocent and the fix could have been so easy. Pride is one of the seven deadly sins, also known as the capital vices or cardinal sins. **Pride** is an inwardly directed emotion that carries two common meanings. With a negative connotation, *pride* refers to an inflated sense of one's personal status or accomplishments, often used synonymously with hubris.

With a positive connotation, *pride* refers to a satisfied sense of attachment toward one's own or another's choices and actions, or toward a whole group of people, and is a product of praise, independent self-reflection, or a fulfilled feeling of belonging.

Additionally, the other six are wrath, greed, sloth, lust, envy, and gluttony. When it came to her I was "guilty" of all 7. I've exuded many different levels of these sins during the course of our relationship, but let's stick with pride for now. Because these are known as the origin of sins, a person should get these things under control to use as the foundation for his/her life. "I don't have this one under control."

Let me tell you about a "falling out" we had that I should have handled better with less display of pride. She owned a king-size, large framed bed with an extremely heavy mattress. She wanted it moved from one room in her house to another. Well, I had already undergone hernia surgery for trying to play the hero to my ex by moving an entire apartment alone, so getting help with that task was a number one priority.

I told her to leave it up to me and off I went to the local Home Depot store to pick up some workers! I got two of them for $10.00 an hour. I explained to them what I needed, informed them of the pay I could afford and together we went back to the house to get the job done. We had to completely disassemble the bed and take it out the front door and into the door of where she wanted it. We finished in an hour's time! The job went smoothly, at least that was what I thought.

I left to take the workers back to their prospective destinations and I got a call from her in total disarray. Apparently we put the mattress on upside down. To me, a basic plea of ignorance and an apology would have sufficed as a suitable response, so that's what I gave, but that wasn't enough. I triggered her anger when I made the statement, "It's just a mattress." She felt like I didn't value her stuff and I made it worse because I didn't return to her house to flip the mattress over.

She laid into me as if the world was falling down. I attempted to calm her with **"words of affirmation,"** we will discuss the love languages in more detail in a later chapter. Nothing I said was good enough, but that's because I just didn't know what to say. We were on the phone, so I couldn't sooth her with the "good d**k." I tried to explain that it was just a mistake and not done intentionally, but that didn't matter either.

All she knew was that it was wrong and if I wasn't gonna do it right, then I should have left it alone for her to do it herself. At that moment, I abandoned every biblical quality that had been embedded in me since the day I was born. Patience was out the window and understanding was on an extended one-way trip to nowhere.

Let's define and expand on the other sins. **Sloth** is defined as spiritual or emotional apathy, neglecting what God has spoken, and being physically and emotionally inactive. Sloth can also indicate a wasting due to lack of use, concerning a person, place, thing, skill, or intangible ideal that would require maintenance, refinement, or support to continue to exist.

She believes as God said that the man is the head of the house and the woman is the helpmate. She doesn't even ask to be number 1. She feels that falling in at number 3, behind God and Man is a rightful place for her to be. One of her biggest complaints, however, about me was that I didn't sex her up, touch her, talk to her, wined her, dined her and spend quality time with her enough. In short, I didn't show her enough attention.

That wasn't my motivation. Yielding from the Albert Einstein quotes, Insanity is doing the same thing over and over again and expecting different results. Well, I guess I must be insane… I have been married three times and in two serious relationships between those. Now, some may look at that and say that I am a very committed man.

Others may feel that there's something wrong with me because I can't keep a relationship. While yet some others may feel that I am insane. Six out of seven women from my past accused me of cheating on them with my work. They all said my business is my mistress and none of them knows each other. Can that statement have any truth to it?

I had gone through some very difficult hard times financially and I hadn't quite mastered the gift of forgiving and forgetting. Therefore, I went into the relationship with blinders on. She was so loving, thoughtful, forgiving, caring and faithful, while I was untrusting, cold, selfish, unforgiving and thoughtless. She would have been happy with just going for walks in the park or having picnics with items purchased from the Dollar Tree.

I was so hung up on not having money that I didn't realize that my love was all the revenue she wanted. If I had my "house in order," then all of those fogged up windows would have been crystal clear.

For Valentine's Day, 2013, she took me to Blue Ridge Mountain to spend the weekend in a cabin. Oh my God! It was the bomb! I have been living in Atlanta for 11 years and talking about it ever since I arrived but have never gone. She comes along and just because I mentioned it to her once, she surprises me with a four day trip to the largest and nicest cabin they have.

Let me tell you all about it. This took some extremely meticulous planning and I must admit that she did an excellent job at pulling it off. My instructions from her were to pack lightly with only two bags, outdoor shoes and some sweatpants, then be outside, ready to go at 2:00 pm sharp on Thursday, February 14th 2013; I complied.

At precisely 2:00 pm a white, stretch, SUV limousine arrived to pick me up. She was seated inside with red rose petals spread all over the seat. The driver placed my bags in the back and off we headed to a surprise weekend getaway. That same day at the same time, President Barrack Obama had arrived at Dobbins Air Reserve Base and several roads were shut down.

I pretended that the roads were closed for me and I gloated as we took the alternate route to head out to our destination. I spent the entire two hour ride frowning because of some silly disagreement we had a few days before. I always told her from day one that, "it doesn't matter what we discuss; it's how you say it that makes the difference." That was the biggest problem between us; her harsh tongue. We were like oil and water. Nevertheless, the trip was off the chain!

She intricately planned and prepared for every little detail. We had to take everything to survive for four days in the mountains without internet, cell or landline phones, or transportation. She coordinated 3 meals, snacks and entertainment for each day. I even received a little gift and a card with every meal. She even hired a masseuse to come out on Saturday to give us both full-body massages.

The cabin slept 9, so we had several different beds to consummate our passion in. There was a pool table of which we played strip-pool, a foosball table, a Jacuzzi, that we played in naked every day and un-curtained windows that only the wild deer had privy to watching us have butt-naked sex on every sofa inside the house and on top of the picnic table outside on the porch.

It was truly one of the top two most wonderful vacations that I had ever been blessed to go on. That weekend, Sloth was definitely not a part of our environment. However, Lust certainly made its way into the arena. **Lust** is an emotion or feeling of intense "desire" in the body. The lust can take any form such as the lust for knowledge, the lust for sex or the lust for power. It can take such mundane forms as the lust for food as distinct from the need for food. Lust is a powerful psychological force producing intense wanting for an object, or circumstance fulfilling the emotion.

My lust for her extended way past sex. I'm somewhat of a dreamer and through the years, my life was constantly messed up because I could never seem to stay in touch with reality. She drew me into her with her overwhelmingly strong convictions. I lusted for her drive, I lusted for her determination and her sense of deeply rooted need to be loved. In her and through her I could see all the things that I was lacking as a man.

The easiest thing in the world to do is "quit." I never learned anything from my mistakes in the past because I didn't stick around long enough to face or correct what was wrong. With her, I became so ruffled that it motivated me to stay so I could get back at her, instead of comprehending that the energy I was wasting trying to get back at her should have gone into correcting the problem and strengthening my foundation.

Envy (from Latin _invidia_) is a resentment which "occurs when someone lacks another's quality, achievement or possession and wishes that the other lacked it." It is said that the first step to overcoming alcoholism is to admit it. I imagine that rule applies to many other things in life that we have to overcome. As such, I have to admit that I envied her for the tenacity she displayed from week to week as she revealed her earning potential.

I have personally watched her bring in $2-$3,000.00 in a single weekend and I was barely getting $1,500.00 in a month. I envied the way she could regard that money as if it was nothing and to me it was the difference between eating from my refrigerator every day or busting the dollar menu wide open. I envied the fact that she had a loyal and dedicated clientele base and I could barely get people to wait until I was out of the room good before they were talking bad about me. Her spirit made people cling to her and my spirit seemed to make people run away.

The last two sins are perhaps the lessor of all that I committed or were guilty of. **Gluttony**, derived from the Latin _gluttire_ meaning to gulp down or swallow, to over-indulgence and over-consumption of food, drink, or wealth items to the point of extravagance or waste. In some

Christian denominations, it is considered one of the seven deadly sins—a misplaced desire for food or its withholding from the needy.

The only thing that I ever exuded gluttony for when it came to her was my enormous desire to tame her. It became an obsession for me, and finally **Greed** is the inordinate desire to possess wealth, goods, or objects of abstract value with the intention to keep it for one's self, far beyond the dictates of basic survival and comfort. It is applied to a markedly high desire for and pursuit of wealth, status, and power.

To love the soul of a black woman, you must first "know" the soul of a black woman. So how do you know when you know? Well, if I would have stopped being so stubborn and just listened to her, I would have acknowledged that she was telling me every day. In the beginning of our relationship she used to greet me with a huge smile and a kiss every time she saw me. She would throw me hints by asking me how my day was and instead of picking up on the signals that she wanted me to do the same and allow her to express her feelings to me, I would just go on and on about my business. She always listened patiently and when I was all talked out she would just accept it and move right along. All she really wanted was to tell me about her day and what was going on in her life.

Day after day, time after time I ran my mouth about things that I did or wanted to do and she never complained. Every crazy scheme that I wanted to try she was always right there by my side, actively involved, and the more I neglected her the less enthusiastic she became about being there for me. It was always about me. I remember one day she asked me a series of questions to see how well I knew her and I only got 3 out of 7 correct.

That's less than half! The sad part is that we talked about those things before. Her favorite color is **brown**, she is **spiritual**, her shoe size is **8**, her favorite movie is **The Color Purple**, her favorite food is **rice**, her favorite pastime is **running**, she is allergic to pineapples, strawberries & morphine, she has a phobia of spiders, she was once bitten by a brown recluse and her favorite person is Maya Angelou. Man, hindsight is 20/20!

I pride myself on being to some extent a "shade tree" philosopher. I'm just full of quotes, logic and sayings. Earlier I mentioned "words of affirmation," which is a part of the five love languages. I used that one because she told me early on that it was her love language. In her youthful years she was always quieted with gifts. She rarely heard, "I love you, or it will be okay." Instead, she was showered with presents, so she rebelled against those actions in her adult life. Maya Angelou said, **"The first time someone shows you who they are, believe them."**

Monee' showed me so many times who she is and I didn't believe her. Actually, I just didn't listen. I replaced a leaky faucet on her kitchen sink once and she got upset with me. She said, "You drove 23 miles just to fix a sink? The handyman can do that." She later told me that she cried when I left. At the time I couldn't understand why she felt some kind of way about that, but now I know that her feet were hurting from standing all day and she preferred that I spend that time and energy massaging her feet and listening to her tell me about why they were in so much pain.

Maya Angelou also said, **"I've learned that people will forget what you said, people will forget what you did, but people will never forget how you made them feel."** That should motivate every man in the world to do whatever he has to do to remember because one of the worst mistakes that a man can make is to forget what a woman says. I agree with Maya that people do remember how you make them feel. In many cases it's called intuition, but it is extremely important to women to be made to feel important. It doesn't matter how small the topic may seem; if you're not talking about God, or something that the Bible said, then your focus should be to be able to repeat back what she says. That makes them happy.

Stephen R. Covey said, **"Most people do not listen with the intent to understand; they listen with the intent to reply."** Monee' possesses a quality that I truly believe is shared by few. The ability to think ahead, anticipate a response and listen with the intent to understand. Many women want to be what she is, but sadly they're greatly confused because they are influenced by television personalities and there are not enough true role models to emulate that are reachable in day to day life.

Let me give you an example. Monee' sometime feels that she is a man living in a woman's body because of her talent to run a household, raise children alone and pay bills each month. However, she has absolutely no desire to do any of it. She wants to be at home, tending to the children and homely duties, cooking, cleaning, doing laundry and anticipating the arrival of her husband.

Monee' enjoys allowing me to sit down, put my feet up and permitting her to remove my shoes, then once I am settled into my chair she brings me dinner, I lead her in prayer and we eat together. She tells me how her day went and how much she missed me and I reciprocate with minimal emphasis on my negative feelings. My purpose is to always ensure that I remain the strong one and that my issues never outweigh hers. She is to be embraced and I am to be encouraged. She is pampered and I am praised. She is to be protected and I am to be promoted. It is when we veer off the beaten path that the road is too rocky to travel.

Steven R. Covey also said, **"Start with the end in mind."** How do you know when you know? Simple, ask yourself, "what is the end?" The answer is judgment day, but of course the more tangible and realistic reply is candidly "death." So how do we determine what we should be like before death? Again, it's simple; the Bible.

Just as I mentioned the seven deadly sins and what the aftermath of violating them could be, the Bible tells us how we should live. Where humans get confused is, "God created us of our own free will," and sure if we sin, then confess and repent he forgives us. The bible says that we should forgive our brother seven times seven but does that mean he should just keep committing the same offense because he knows that he will be forgiven?

Being created of our own free will means we have the "choice" of doing the right thing. In any given situation in order for someone to be right, someone has to be wrong, which makes us stand apart. However, if we both stand on the ground of righteousness, then we can stand together. It's not always so important to be right! The bible is the common bind of righteousness and through it we can reach the soul of the black woman.

Things have changed so much over the years, but one thing that will never go away is the roots that bond the black family together and that's religion. Although you may see women of today leaving the club and showing up in Church wearing the same dress from the previous night out, they still hold it together through prayer.

"There's nothing you can say or do to take back something that you say or do." jb brown. Your mouth will only speak what your heart and mind allows. Reading the bible will certainly fill you with the Holy Ghost and it will definitely familiarize you with the scriptures and all the right things to say, but you still have to effectively deploy that "free will" we talked about. It is almost impossible not to be exposed to the world and the corrupted society that we live in.

Damn near every television show you watch today will have a considerable amount of cursing in it, but does that mean that just because it was said on TV that a man has to call a woman a bitch? What about women who curse like sailors? Women like to be called Angels but how many people actually know that there were no female Angels? You hear the black woman say, "I want to be treated like a queen, but it's hard to treat someone like a queen who has the manners of a goat and the grace of a bull."

Sisters, please don't think that you're without fault. You want to join your man and his boys for poker night, tailgate with him or Monday night football. You grab your crotch, slapping high-five or giving the "man-hug", drink beer, burp and yell louder than most of the men in the room, then you turn around with the same voice and say to your man, "You don't treat me like a lady." Again, I know times have changed but you just can't have it both ways. How do Proverbs feel about a "lady" behaving that way? What if your lady is not a religious woman, then what, fellas?

Then you have to make the determination in the beginning if you are right for "each other." I know that the physical can be overwhelming sometimes but why force yourself to be with someone that you know you really don't want? I know; loneliness, right? Here's the problem with that, with change comes change (Remember Newton's third law?) and if you're not willing to change, then you can't expect him or her to change for you and it just won't work!

It wasn't hard at all to determine that my love language is "Quality of Time" as demonstrated through my constant desire to be around her. I'd spend hours at her place of business and I often asked her to join me at mine. I also loved when she went to class with me or just stopped by for a visit unannounced. The problem with my love language was that I "hogged" all the time.

I sub-conscientiously manipulated her into spending all her time with me and I didn't give equal consideration to the things she liked to do. I organized seven different events that she unselfishly attended and was actively involved with.

I can't think of a time that I wanted to do something that she was not more eager to do than I was. I don't believe that people only fall under one specific love language and the rest don't affect them. I mean, most women love receiving gifts, but Monee' couldn't care less about a present without a big dose of words and love attached.

I feel that Monee' possessed all of the love languages but allowed me to again reflect upon a time when I should have given her more "words of affirmation" but instead I chose to say the wrong thing once again and the shit really hit the fan. May 29th 2013, mid-afternoon at her place of business. I had to retrieve some items from my thumb-drive and I walked away with the drive still in her computer. She began using the computer, looked in my files and saw several pictures, one of which was a shot of a female and me.

"Who is that in this picture with you?" She asked with a slight snarl on her face and continued to flip through the photos. I positioned myself to see the computer screen then replied, "Oh, that's Rachel. We went to my award ceremony together a couple of years ago." "Why is she backing it up on you like that?" She asked, as her grimace became more and more menacing. "It's just a pose." I replied." "It didn't mean anything." "Did you have sex with her?" She interrogated, with an all-out frown. "**What difference does it make?** That was two years ago."

Bam! That's where I made my mistake. The **"Words of Affirmation"** that she was looking for was, "No, Baby. Listen, that was the first and last time she and I ever did anything together. There was NO sex. I never even saw her again after that. She had a new dress and nowhere to go and I had an event with no date, so we went together. That's all. You have nothing to worry about. I'm with you and I should have destroyed those pictures a long time ago."

Instead, my pride took me down the wrong path and she flew into a rage that prompted her to begin punching, kicking and throwing things. I abandoned the small piece of philosophy consisting of two small words that I truly believe could save every man's relationship and perhaps his life at some point and those words are, **"Okay, Baby."** Closely followed by 2 more, **"You're right and Yes, Dear."**

DISCUSSION QUESTION—SHOULD YOU ANNOUNCE YOUR PET PEEVES BEFORE THEY HAPPEN, AS THEY'RE HAPPENING OR NOT AT ALL?

CHAPTER IV

"KNOW WHAT SHE WANTS"

I had seen her upset before but this was different. Her fury was damn near as if someone had stolen one of her children. She struck items with total disregard to her knuckles and skin. I stared for a moment in disbelief, and then attempted to calm her, but it was too late. That situation resulted from me not practicing and deploying 3 essential elements. **1.** Remember I said, "There's nothing you can say or do to take back something that you say or do?" Well, this was proof positive! **2.** Learn to listen. Monee' told me several times throughout our relationship, "Give me words of affirmation." **3.** "Just be honest with me."

Truthfully, that whole thing could have been avoided if I had just deleted those damned pictures before I met her. I didn't need those pictures. Rachel meant absolutely nothing to me. We didn't touch beyond taking the pictures, kiss, have sex or even hold hands, but yet I held on to pictures that violated the trust and confidence that Monee' had in me and there was never even any hope or desire of Rachel and I being together in a romantic way.

LESSON 4, "BE RIGHTEOUS; "ALL" RIGHT?"

At the time of the aforementioned situation I felt like actions didn't warrant her reaction, but I keep forgetting that we are not programmed like robots. We were created of our own free will; therefore we have to program ourselves. When you implant a way of life in your heart, pray about it, read the bible and practice those standards every day, then it comes out automatically in heated moments. You have to ask yourself, fellas, "What am I gaining from this?" Nonetheless, let's explore further as to what it means.

Statistics suggest that the number one cause of breakups and divorce is finances; I disagree. I believe that the number one cause of break ups is **"lack of or poor communication."** What are some common issues in relationships? Infidelity, abuse, incompatibility, opposing career goals, opposing ideas regarding child rearing or raising, social differences, finances and of course, communication. Of all the things listed, communication is the one thing that can bond all the others. With good, open, honest communication we can compromise about any issue, including finances. We are just so damn stubborn and prideful; no one ever wants to be wrong, but we've talked about that, right?

When we move on from a relationship there is no need of hanging on. Nothing good comes from living in the past, so if I had gotten rid of those pictures of Rachel and me after our relationship resolved, which was nothing more than a night of convenience out together, and that entire fiasco could have been avoided, but hold on, there's more; I didn't quit there.

I flew out to Texas the next morning for four days and for the duration of that time Monee' and I didn't speak. I avoided her calls and told her through texting that I did not desire to speak to her. I was acting like a little bitch. I once again made up my mind that I was done with that relationship.

I returned on Sunday, which was the third consecutive day of no interaction with Monee', and selfishly and inappropriately secured a ride home from a female associate. Of course I was later accused of screwing her, but once again in hindsight I admit that too could have been avoided if I had communicated better with Monee'. The fourth day came and finally she reached out to me. "I think it was very rude and disrespectful for you to go 4 days without speaking to me," She texted. "You're right; it was,"

I replied, then one of us, I don't recall who, followed up with a call.

We indulged in a very intense conversation that lasted upwards of 45 minutes. She requested that I come to her home after work to talk things out; I agreed. She had designed a very elaborate chart denoting her interpretation of how relationships should work and I was very impressed with her philosophy and approach. We again decided to give it another try and continue. Once again we were at peace, another battle won, but the problem was that I didn't take the time then to prepare for the war. A close Pastor friend of mine told me once,

LESSON 5, "DON'T TAKE AWAY YOUR KINDNESS."

Monee' is a social butterfly who could just walk into a room and instantly command the attention of everyone there; both men and women. She can make friends with strangers and have men wanting to take her home and women wanting to be her friend within minutes. The wonderful thing about it though is I wasn't made to feel left out, neglected or disrespected. It's funny, with all of the attention that she got from others; all she really wanted was attention from me.

She honored me by going to an "old school" party with me one Saturday night. We had such a wonderful time and as usual, unintentionally, she became the center of attention. An old white guy came over to us and asked her to dance. Normally I would have caught an attitude with him, but for once, although I was still a bit jealous, I was understanding. Besides, he was old and could barely stand up, so I didn't feel a threat.

She did tell me that she loves to dance and I did love dancing with her. There was a natural glow that emanated from her that made me constantly think about sexing her up and she was mine, so I can only imagine how other guys felt when they looked at her. Things were very peaceful between us that night and I regret not getting down on my knees and thanking God for the gift that he had given me.

That would have kept me connected to the foundation and put me in the conscious state of mind to dig up the old roots and clean out the old attics. I should have never befriended the female associate that took me home from the airport.

If only I had listened to Monee'… The woman told me how to love her. She all but took me by the hand and led me to the classroom, but **"I didn't listen!"** If nothing else I say in this book sticks with you or means anything, please remember, **"Learn to listen."** Monee' is a beautiful woman and a beautiful person that naturally attracts people. I was so jealous of her that I ended up running off all of her friends. I wanted her all to myself but I didn't supplement the things that I forced her to get rid of. She likes the bar life and I don't.

I have this preconceived notion that females that go to the bar alone are just there to flirt, be seen and taken home for sex. Monee' told me that was not the case with her; she just liked the atmosphere, the challenging conversation and freedom of expanding her lifestyle so that her social life is not so boring.

LESSON 6, "YOU CAN THROW A FEATHER, BUT A ROCK MIGHT BE THROWN BACK AT YOU."

However due to my selfishness and lack of trust, all I heard was blah, blah, blah… One of my old partners used to say that all the time. I've never researched to see if that was a famous quote by some philosopher, but it holds equal value to me either way.

Sometimes listening even means listening to yourself. After my divorce from my third wife I wrote a "spoken word" piece to release some of my frustration behind what happened. Although the words are exceptionally powerful, I didn't follow my own philosophy and apply the things to Monee'. I'd like to share that piece with you all and let you judge for yourself.

2 DEGREES PAST LOVIN' YOU

I was 2 degrees past lovin'
you,

3 degrees past hating you.

I was 4 degrees past kicking your
ass,

and less than 1 degree close to killing you!

You stood in front of God and you bowed to Thee

You vowed to me

Promised to love, honor and cherish for eternity

For better or for worse, til death due us part

Then you gave another woman what God made to be

All the little things you said men wouldn't do

Girl, I did for you,

I wanted you to know that my love was true

I would kill for you

Die for you

In every little crisis I would guide us through

You were my boo. I was 2 Degrees Past Lovin' You.

Just to see your smile I used to read to you

Girl, I would bleed for you

Promised to spend my whole life just pleasing you

Swore to protect you from danger

I was touched by an Angel

Girl, I could see the Della Reese in you

At no single time did I ever lie

I'd rather pluck out my eyes than to see you cry

Feels like you ripped out my heart

And my world fell apart

Just the thought of you gone made me wanna die

I'd place the world at your feet just to have a kiss

Just to feel the bliss

I don't know how to be lonely

cause I'm new to this

I've tried to face the realization

That you have a new sensation

Where my hips used to be

Now her face exist

Adam and Eve was God's first design

He had us in mind

I'm pretty sure it was meant to stay that way throughout time

I just don't understand why a woman wants to be a man

And wear a plastic penis twice as big as mine

To try to love again I had uncertainty

Although I certainly

Thank God for blessing thee

With the wisdom and the love he instilled in me

Extra long days watching the price is right

Spending night after night

Realizing that I'm no longer young or restless

As my world continues to turn and turn

Hoping I can learn, "Something 'bout the way you make me feel, oh, oh, oh" Is this for real?

See I meant what I said when I said, "I do"

Cause you were my boo

I was already 2 Degrees Past Lovin' You

Now I'm happy to say that I have a new. A true boo

Everything I've dreamed of I have in you

With you in my life I have eternity and stability

I'll never hold you accountable for what she did to me

I even yearn for the taste of your teardrop

I don't wanna see you cry but babe I can't stop

I'm not meant to be single so I'll stand strong

Like an old song

If lovin' you ain't right

Just let me be wrong

I was 2 degrees past lovin' her

But with you in my life she is just a blur

She can't even hold a candle to how you make me feel

I will always love, honor, cherish and baby keep it real

I hope you're 2 degrees past lovin' me

Cause what I wanna see with you and me is 2 degrees past Eternity. I'm done!

That was written more than a year before I met Monee', so what the hell happened? She told me several times during our relationship that she enjoys being read to, but yet I never did it, and it wasn't until another dude took her to a park, sat on a swing and read to her that I even attempted to try. What about that line, "All the little things you said men wouldn't do, I would do for you, cause I wanted you to know that my love was true?" If I really wanted her to know that my love was true, then she would never have to ask me to do anything because it would be done automatically without words.

When a woman hears a man write or speak those words you have to remember that is like the ultimate nonphysical attraction that compels women to men and we have to be ready to back it up. Getting that ride from the female associate stripped away Monee's privilege, pleasure and right to be there for me; it was an inappropriate display of intimacy because I affectionately leaned on someone else in my moment of despair, regardless of how pissed off she may have been in previous days or moments.

Anything that you allow another woman to do for you places a wedge between you and your desired one; especially if feelings are involved. Any time that is spent with another woman is time taken away from your love. Any thought that is directed towards another person is a thought your love is deprived of.

June 13th 2013, yet again, due to my selfishness and wrong choice, sinful pride and poor communication, I allowed an innocent occurrence to detonate into another disruption. At a daytime office social gathering my female associate brought a pound cake to be shared. Unfortunately, no one partook in eating any of it, so she asked me to take it home because she had to go straight to work and she could pick it up from me later.

LESSON 7, "WHAT'S THE VALUE."

I put the cake in my refrigerator and thought nothing of it. Wrong choice! Monee', because she listens, knew that I loved pound cake. I actually thought that the cake would be gone before Monee' returned to my apartment and she would never know about it, but it wasn't picked up that night. Initially, she assumed it belonged to me, so she disregarded it and I didn't tell her otherwise. So, did I lie? Damn right I did! Let's discuss that further a little later.

I allowed my associate to come by and pick up the cake a day later and she insisted that I take a slice for myself. Later that night Monee' came over and noticed that the cake was gone and only a large slice remained. Through some mild questioning I finally revealed the details of where the cake came from and who it belonged to. No dice! By this time, as far as she was concerned I was a lying sack of shit and she was about to deal with it.

Why didn't I just say I couldn't take the cake home? That would have voided everything, but stupidity triumphed and my wits were conquered by the grips of deception. When will I ever learn? "What was the value?" I got nothing out of bringing that cake home. I didn't even get to eat my slice because Monee' dumped it in a bowl in the sink and filled it with dish water. As I said before, **"You may throw a feather but a rock may get thrown back at you."**

That single action of bringing home a freaking cake triggered a multitude of reactions that culminated into an avalanche. Before I met Monee' I used to pride myself on being 100% honest with my lady, but I don't think I've lied so much to all of my exes combined as to equal or exceed how much I lied to her. There's a statement that unquestionably needs an explanation attached. **"Avoiding the truth doesn't make it untrue and it doesn't make it go away."** jb brown. One of the things that I was most proud of in my most previous relationships was the unequivocal leverage I give myself to be totally honest with them.

Of course this meant some sacrifice on my part as well. It meant that I couldn't do anything wrong, but that wasn't such a bad thing. I had done so much wrong in the past anyway that I had grown way past being tired of it. The feeling was awesome! It just seemed to fit like a glove. I really don't know what compelled me to put myself in so many little situations that caused me to lie to her or keep things from her. The amazing part about it was that I always got busted or told on myself.

Despite the ugly outcome of the cake circumstances I stupidly and selfishly maintained a line of communication with the female associate. I assigned her a specific ringtone in my phone. I wasn't thinking about this song being of a sexual nature when I connected it. I just associated the personality with the music. Big mistake! That seems to be becoming a bad habit, doesn't it? Monee' and I were at her place of business again in July and my young associate called.

The ringtone was very pronounced this time as my phone was turned up loud and in close proximity. "Why didn't you answer your phone? Who is that calling you?" Monee' abruptly inquired. "Oh, that's just Lauren. We're talking. I can call her later." I confidently, yet cautiously replied. "Why does she have such a sexual ringtone?" "Call her back!" Screwing up has become a familiar pattern for me and the fireworks commenced.

I still recall our first argument. Remember I said it's not always so important to be right? Well, I designed this hoodie and Monee' got her Mother to help me out by sewing the hoods on. She and I went to pick up the fabric and we got into what started out to be a discussion about how much cloth to get. She stated that it would take ¾ of a yard to make one hood; therefore 10 yards would make 10 hoods. I disagreed and said, actually 10 yards would make 12 hoods because there would be a quarter yard left from each one, so for every fourth yard there would be one additional yard.

Saying that was another wrong decision! "No it won't!" she proclaimed quite forcefully. "My Mother has been sewing since I was a child and she's worked for some of the biggest celebrities in the business, so she knows exactly what it takes!" "I'm not disputing that." I replied passionately. "I'm just doing the math." "That's your problem… You think you know everything! I'm trying to help you and you just have to be right!" She continued.

That is where I made my first big mistake. I should have asked myself, "What's the value?" It meant absolutely nothing for me to prove to her that 10 yards would make 12 hoods. Instead, I should have been thanking her for contacting her Mother on my behalf and praising her for having my back. The aftermath from that explosion was nowhere near worth me being right.

I was 46 years old when I met Monee' and I had never once, through all of my relationships, been told that. She hit me with the, "A real man won't take away his kindness no matter what a woman does." Of course, my big mouth had to come back with, "A real woman would put a man in the position to do so." That just led to more yelling and cursing. She asked me to take her back home to get her vehicle and when we arrived she didn't kiss me good-bye and I didn't get out to walk her to the car and open the door.

I drove away with my mind made up to drop her. I organized a shoot the next evening and did not tell her about it. It involved a female actress and me in a bedroom scene. Although there were four other people there, I was still accused of having sex with the actress. I do understand why Monee' felt that way. We exchanged some additional harsh words on the phone and I told her that I needed to speak to her in person.

She already knew what I was going to say and insisted that I not waste time and gas driving 23 miles just to tell her it was over. I drove anyway because I didn't want to break up over the phone. After extensive and intense conversation between us, I decided to give it another try but asserted that she fix her attitude. She would go from 0-60 in 4.3 seconds and I would spend hours trying to figure out what I did wrong or what I could do to prevent it from happening again.

That was perhaps the fastest progression through the 5 stages of grief that I had ever seen. She was in denial from the moment she stepped out of my car. She tried her best to pretend that she didn't care, so the silent treatment began. We spent the rest of the day and half of the next not speaking at all. The anger came multiple times and seemed to grow stronger with each passing moment between us.

She bargained with herself for several hours and did a considerable amount more with me once she surrendered to the feelings that had taken over her emotions. She confessed of her depression, though her voice, tears and actions were a dead giveaway. Finally, acceptance swooped in and it was time to react. That's when the pleading began. I felt like I had been issued a grand challenge and no matter how tough it became I had to stick it out and rise to the occasion.

Maslow has a hierarchy of needs that serve as the foundation for human awareness. I took it upon myself to assess those categories and how they applied to Monee' and me. Beginning at the bottom with our physiological needs I ascertained that her needs far outweighed mine. This level includes breathing, food, water, homeostasis, sex and sleep. Of course there's also shelter, clothing and simply human interaction.

We both thoroughly enjoyed having sex with each other. I had three exes that gave it up two-three times a day. One of them I could just walk out of the room and come back and she looked new to me and I'd want her again, but it stretches way beyond intercourse. However Monee's physiological needs are strongly inclusive of all aspects of the physiological sense.

For example, she insists on getting a full 8 hours of sleep, while I only 4-6. She consumes 6-8 bottles of water each day and she had to damn near kill me to make me drink one. She likes organic food and vegetables, no pork, sugar or excessive beef, and I don't like vegetables or organic foods. The mind and body have to be balanced as with homeostasis, which is extremely important to Monee' and me.

As for shelter and clothing it is important to both of us to be comfortable where we call home and that our cloths are clean and they fit but the slight difference is I am way more anal about order and tidiness. She says I have OCD, I just think I am OC without the D.

The second level is Safety. It's strange how we go day to day being totally oblivious to our surroundings. We used to have intense conversations about living in a gated community. Oddly enough I prefer it and she wants people to be able to come right up unrestricted up to her door. I'm ex-military, so I'm used to being surrounded and protected. She, on the other hand, considers herself to be a "free spirit" and is all about honesty and freedom.

I sat around and slept with my handgun and constantly plotted ways of countering a drive-by, home invasion, or parking lot attack and she would go to sleep with the door unlocked. I do understand her way of thinking, though. Women want the man to take care of keeping the home safe while they keep their minds free to take care of domestic responsibilities.

The thing about Monee' that differed so much from the average woman was that she wanted to be domestic. The common, liberal woman of today desires to stand among men. I totally disagree with women competing with men. I feel that God created women the way he intended them to be. This includes the way women walk, talk, look, smell, taste, laugh, smile, cry, kiss and most of all reproduce. Anytime we change what we are naturally, we fiddle with God's design.

Take a car for example, why would time, money, and energy go into engineering and building a vehicle if it was okay to drive it patched up with "duct tape."

The human body is perhaps one of the most complex creations ever constructed. I can recall when I was growing up other children wanting to have their tonsils taken out or someone being okay with having their appendix removed. Do they live on without those organs? Sure, but is that the way God intended it to be? I don't think so.

Wanting a man to "do the right thing" is perfectly okay, but I need you to remember this. He that is without sin let him cast the first stone. John 8:7 KJV. Ladies, you can't expect a man to be worried about cleaning up for you if you haven't swept around your own back door.

Men have gotten past the physical changes, the liberal behavior, and the sports barriers, but is it really asking too much to tone down the attitudes? Today's black woman has taken the hand on the hip, neck rolling, and finger pointing to an entirely new level. There is nothing wrong with being expressive, strong and passionate about your beliefs or standards, but it doesn't have to be so abrasive. The mean mugging, frowning and staring down are all unnecessary. Ladies, we know what you want; it's just our damned stupid pride and stubbornness that stops us from giving it to you. Guess what? We also know what we want.

The NBA, National Basketball Association, The WBA, Women's Basketball Association, WWC, World Wrestling Confederation, local bowling league and book clubs are just a few examples of organizations that people are a part of. We all want to be loved and belong to something or someone, which is the 3rd stage of Maslow's Hierarchy of Needs. No matter how far away they roam, church and religion will always bring the black woman back home. If that's true, brothers, then why is it so hard for us to determine what makes them happy? That's an easy one fellas; they don't always want to stand on the right side of right. What the hell does that mean?

Remember my spoken word piece, *"2 Degrees Past Lovin' You?"* Let me remind you of a passage, **"I just don't understand why a woman wants to be a man, and wear a plastic penis twice as big as mine."** Again, we are created of our own free will. This crap about, "I'm really tired of men treating me bad! They are such liars! I will never be with another man because they're no good!" BS!

Ladies, you get with other women because you like the feeling you get from touching, licking, rubbing and kissing the right spots in the right way! It has nothing to do with us being liars or treating you badly. I have personally witnessed stud women going off on their female, "fem," counterpart, smashing the cellphone, trashing the car and even physical abuse.

Somebody please explain this one to me. A woman decides to get with another woman because she hates "men," and the woman she gets with dresses like a man, wears a haircut like a man, deepens her voice to sound like a man, walks like a man, wears a strap-on penis or packs a sock in her drawers, straps down her breasts, won't let the female see, touch, lick or suck them and goes into the men bathroom. How the hell does that make sense?

My brain can't even process some stupid shit like that! If you choose to be with a woman, then be with a woman! I still disagree but at least you're being truthful about what you really want.

I went home one day to an ex, Ruth, and to my surprise there was another female there with her. The female was someone that we knew and had been trying to get with Ruth for more than 4 months. She was a somewhat attractive lady, who said that she had only been with one man all her life. I greeted both of them and continued in the back room to allow the two of them to continue their "girl-talk." Moments later, Ruth entered the room and said to me, "Veronica said she wants to watch."

Suffering from a momentary spell of Idiocy I replied, "Watch what?" "Us!" She disclosed with a slight grin. "Us?

Oh! You mean, us? Okay, well I have two conditions…" I said as her grin turned into a full-blown laugh and Ruth closed the door to preserve face. "First, I want her to say it to me herself and secondly, after we're done I want to watch the two of you." "Okay, I'll ask her. "Ruth replied and was excited to take my demands to her horny friend. A moment later she returned with a verbal confirmation of Veronica's willingness to comply.

I returned to the front room and Veronica surrendered the words I requested and the games began! Veronica volunteered to slowly remove Ruth's clothes as I reciprocated with the gradual dismounting of my own. Ruth and I engaged in a long, slow, adoring kiss as a dual set of hands began an unimpeded exploration of my body. Nipples were stiffened, veins were pulsating, eyes were gleaming and we suddenly found ourselves in a "tri-kiss." There were two tongues in my mouth, 4 hands on my body and 2 wet vaginas, hot and ready, like CeCe's Pizza impatiently waiting for me to make my selection.

Overwhelmed by the constant friction and progressive sexual tension, Veronica sensually unclothed herself and generously exposed her voluptuous body. I felt like I was in a smorgasbord and I brought my appetite. Her breasts were tight, erect and firm. Her stomach was flat and her frame was shaven with no visible marks. Her odor was pleasant and fresh like a bouquet of newly picked roses, dethorned, arranged and ready to be given as a beautiful Valentine's Day gift. I found myself equally balanced between my love for Ruth and the quickly accumulated lust I developed for Veronica.

With her legs gapped open widely, Veronica aggressively fingered herself as I pounded Ruth into the sandwich that Veronica and I made out of her. After 15-20 minutes of antagonizing Veronica, I finally inserted myself inside Veronica. She moaned from desire and I countered each tone with an additional thrust. There was no doubt that it was what she wanted, at least for the moment. Veronica wanted to sex Ruth so badly that she sacrificed her long-term abstinence from men just to have a few moments of belly rubbing, coochie grinding female action.

This untamed action went on for quite some time, then I selfishly withdrew myself, sat across on the other sofa and watched the two of them ferociously unleash unrestricted desire as if the end of the world had just been announced. They kissed, caressed, grinded and gazed at each other like there was no tomorrow. The more I sat there observing, the more turned on I became. Self-discipline was exercised at its greatest peak; I can never remember another time, in any given situation, that I had to deploy that much self-control. It was better than any porn I had ever seen in my life, and this was live! Finally I couldn't take it anymore and rejoined for one last insertion; I think that climax left me in a breathless, sweaty, body-ridged and toes pointed state of weakness, but it was worth every minute.

Esteem comes in at stage 4 on the scale. I consider myself a nice looking dude and in good shape. I am very confident, I have good teeth, smooth skin and all, well most of my hair. I'm relatively intelligent, well read, and a good conversationalist. I've never had problems getting women. I just hate being single. I don't like being alone or I should say, "lonely." I do have my moments when I like some, "me" time; I'm sure everyone does. Confidence shows in a man's attitude, his dress, his chosen words and topics.

Women like a man who's sure of himself. I was at a strip club one afternoon and they were running one of their little gimmicks where men could get a lap-dance for a dollar. I was wearing a button-down vest with no shirt underneath and this "not so attractive" stripper approached me to request a dance. I told her that I didn't have a dollar, so she gave me one and proceeded to bestow upon me an untamed, unsolicited and really unwanted lap-dance. My arrogance commanded attention to the degree of compelling her to pay me to receive what I should have paid her to give.

That, to me, was a clear cut example of low self-esteem. Women often display various bits of evidence as to their uncertainty and it's not always in the form of a pathetic action such as the previous example. Being loud and disruptive is also a reflection of low self-esteem. There is a gross lack of poise being shown from a "lady" who shouts out disrespectful vulgarities just to make a point. Think about it, can you not make the same point without yelling, cursing and showing a nasty attitude? Here's a better question. Is there ever a time when a "lady" has to behave that way? I think not…

Self-Actualization is the 5th and final level of Maslow's stages. I would be remiss not to speak on Monee's remarkable appetite for continuing to stride. She is without a doubt the most self-motivated person that I have ever personally had the pleasure of knowing. She gives new meaning to, "whatever it takes."

Earlier I mentioned my numerous schemes. Well, not once did I initiate something and Monee' ever hesitated at all to jump right in and become an active and intricate part of the process; even if she knew nothing about what I was trying to do, she would perform the functions that she was familiar with.

DISCUSSION QUESTION—HOW MANY TIMES SHOULD YOU TELL A PERSON THAT SOMETHING BOTHERS YOU?

CHAPTER V

"THE EASIEST THING IN THE WORLD TO DO IS QUIT"

Monee' suffers from migraine headaches, to the point that often she has to be hospitalized and administered potent medication to soothe the savage beast. One day while at my home she was stricken with an attack and it was a bad one. She described her pain as being "hit by a train, then run over by a Mack truck." In tears, she mentioned "reflexology" to me and requested that I attempt to find some pressure points on her feet and hands. Pursuant to a brief self-directed crash course taken from the Internet I quickly began vigorously massaging her feet in an effort to seek out these various points of relief.

It was amazing! It was as though I had gone to training for two years to become an expert Reflexologist. Within 5-10 minutes she felt relief. As I followed the instructions and applied my recently gained knowledge she proclaimed the instant relief she felt. Her tears dried up and her frown blossomed into the naturally beautiful smile that emanated the very essence of her soul. That led to

LESSON # 8, "OLD ROOTS BARE FRUIT."

Energized by her newly discovered remedy, she quickly began encouraging me to start my own practice as a Masseuse and Reflexologist. The vibes that emitted from her excitement made it impossible to reject, so I humbly agreed. Immediately she "took the bull by the horn" and formatted a plan.

She developed a mini business plan, designed and ordered business cards, bought a cell phone, created a Craigslist ad and sent out a mass text to several people encouraging them to give me a try by offering to pay for the first session, and that was for "me" to start a business, so just imagine what she does for herself.

I created a dish, an entree called, "Eggs Extraordfamous." Yeah, I know it's not a word; I made it up. As the name suggests, it has an egg base and one of the other ingredients is Shrimp. Of course you know I can't tell you the rest of it, then I'd be giving away my trade secret. At any rate, the second time I invited her to my apartment I figured I'd tone things down a bit by cooking dinner for her.

Off to the kitchen I went stirring, mixing, chopping and frying. It was a masterpiece and I was proud to be the chef. I served it up, we prayed together and down the hatch. It took her several weeks to tell me that she doesn't like eggs or shrimp but because her mission was to please me she ate the dish and never gave off a negative vibe or sign. How is that for self-actualization?

You have to explore every intricate facet of a true black woman's soul in order to reach the core. It makes her feel good, and if you don't show your appreciation, she's not gonna give you the, "F**k it! I don't care!" response that you may have grown accustomed to because the truth is, "she does care." No, you're gonna get the full blown, "I gave you my all and you just shitted on me" attitude because it means the world to her to receive your love as compensation for her giving you hers. A true black woman practices and studies ways of loving her black man, so it's like a spit in her face if you don't properly open up and nourish her love. To her you're just trampling all over her and she's not having it!

A true black woman will open up her heart, mind and world to let you explore so deep that you will feel like you're on an expedition that takes you to the deepest, darkest ends of the earth. When learning to love the soul of a black woman you must get to know every phase of all characteristics of her existence; not just what you see! That is the fuel that keeps her going. It doesn't cost money, trips or jewels, just time, effort and respect on your part. Remember what I told you about the white man respecting the black woman?

The black woman demands respect because she's speaking out and crying out for all of the beautiful black women that came before her who were raped, beaten and made to do things that didn't get her the proper respect but still had to carry the burden of keeping the family together and holding down the household while the black man endured the whips and chains of repression.

It is more intense studying than any college course of any University in the country. "Respect" is a highly misunderstood word that's often taken to mean that a person has low or no regard for another, but respect is a feeling of deep admiration for someone or something elicited by their abilities, qualities, or achievements.

The missing element from the black man is the "deep admiration" for the black woman. It's not that we don't appreciate who the black woman is and what she's gone through, but there are so many layers just to get to the nucleus that we run out of patience before reaching it. In other cases we can't handle what we perceive as a bad attitude so we stop trying. Most of us don't develop a deep admiration for the black woman because we don't fight through the storm or take time to get to know her soul. Perhaps many of us don't even realize that there is so much to the black woman's soul.

Let's take it a step further; if the true definition of respect is "deep admiration," then what is the suitable substitute or viable replacement when making reference to the subject. Example, the father of the house says to his son or daughter, "As long as you live under my roof you will **respect** me!" Translation; "As long as you live under my roof you will "do as I say, follow my rules and conduct yourself the right way!" In that case he is demanding someone to develop a deep admiration for him because he is in charge, a parent or the head of the house.

The black woman, on the other hand, means exactly what it implies. "You will develop a deep admiration for me and it will be elicited by my qualities, abilities and achievements!" Not the achievements you may be thinking of though; The black woman could give a rat's ass about how many sports she played in high school or how many plays or movies that she's been in.

She's earned the respect because a human life is implanted, developed, grown and delivered from her body and that same body continues on to cook, clean, do laundry, take care of the children, comfort everyone and keep her man sexually satisfied. Now if that doesn't deserve some deep admiration, then I don't know what does!

We make so many BS excuses about why we "can't" love a black woman til we don't take heed to how easy it really is. Ladies, please don't believe that you don't play a major part in the taming of a man's mindset to love you the right way! I'm not going to back off of the "Angry black woman syndrome" or the "bad attitude."

What you have to acknowledge is that every man is not the same and you can't blame the next one for the actions of the last one. He is a whole new person and I know that it's draining but if you believe what the bible says in Romans

28, then you must know that the right one for you does exist. Fellas, you have to make the black woman feel like she's the only woman alive that you want.

I can promise you this; if you take the time to appreciate and cherish the way the black woman longs to make you feel, you won't even have an urge to look at another woman, but do us all a favor; if you don't want to reciprocate 100% of what a true black woman is, then move on and let another brother, who does, have her. You will both be happier. You have to take the time to explore the deepest depths of the black woman; otherwise you will never get to know her abilities, qualities or achievements.

The most common phrase that comes from a man's mouth when he sees a woman that he's attracted to is: "Damn, she's fine!" But just what is being fine? Is it the way that a woman is shaped? What about the way she wears her clothes? Or is it the way she walks, talks or smiles? Is being "fine" to one person the same as the next or any other? You know what they say about a man's trash... There are so many different interpretations for someone being "fine," but in reality a black woman's soul holds a fineness all its own and that's why we always come to a screeching halt after we get past the physical.

Of course there has to be somewhat of a mutual attraction, but what about when there's not? Quite often we may see a couple that "in our eyes" don't look right together, but what exactly is "right?" What happens is, the woman is a knockout with the most well-toned body that you would ever want to see and the guy would look like "who done it and why."

So what's really going on? Well, he's wearing a $1,000.00 suit, $750.00 shoes, a $10,000.00 watch, expensive rings and driving a $40,000.00 car, but his personality sucks, his sense of humor is dry, he's not very smart, his breath stinks and he beats the hell out of his woman every other week.

Of course I took it a bit extreme on that description but if that same guy would learn to love the soul of a black woman, he wouldn't develop that demonic craving to hit her; he would see that a true black woman is inherently hungry to uplift her man and she would expose him to a different class of people, teach and guide him to read and study to better his personality, work towards improving his sense of humor, help put him through college, if necessary, and buy him a giant bag of "peppermints." The black woman's soul does not lend itself to compromise; it's the journey to the soul that yields to the route in getting there. So what happens when both people are extremely attractive or atrociously ugly? Does that put them on even grounds?

That's making love to her soul. The constant thrusting of your kindness and understanding striking vigorously against her mental "G-Spot" gives her a psychological erection that is stiffer than a fully grown Oak tree. Fellas, it's not such a daunting task; realize that a woman who is really into you will rarely see the wrong anyway. Ladies, don't allow your negative feelings about your past experiences to ruin a positive opportunity for your future and please don't fool yourself trying to fool your potential mate.

Let me explain; you told your girls that you want to be with a man who is wealthy and that you want to be wined and dined on a regular basis. Okay, there's nothing wrong with wanting to be treated nice, but let's face it, in these trying times how often are you going to meet that perfect guy with all the features you want and he's banking too?

You have the nerve to complain if a guy doesn't take you out to a fancy or expensive restaurant on the first date. You don't know if you and he are going to hit it off! I met a female who told me that taking her to Red Lobster would be an insult. I told her that she had lost her damn mind! As I said before, Red Lobster used to be the premiere spot to go to when the old school romance progressed.

Besides, every woman is not worthy of a $50.00 meal. Hold on ladies, slow your roll! You know I'm speaking the truth. Some of you have spent so much money in McDonald's, Burger King, Wendy's and KFC that you should be part owner, then you act like you're too damn good to eat there just because you meet a man. You can't spend time shopping in Family Dollar if you're looking for a Saks Fifth Avenue type of guy!

Many times in generic conversations I've heard it said that two people should be **"equally yoked."** There's another one of those misunderstood and misused statements. What exactly does that mean? In the Christian community the phrase is a biblical term used mostly to refer to a marriage or relationship.

The phrase **"unequally yoked"** doesn't particularly refer to marriage. In fact, the saying "equally yoked" is not even in the bible. **II Corinthians 6:14** (KJV) says, "Be ye not unequally yoked with unbelievers. . ." It doesn't say relationships, it doesn't say marriage but its inference is that of any relationship with another person. A relationship with another person could be a business partnership.

Do you have any idea how simple it is to make a black woman smile? You can just notice a new pair of shoes, earrings, or a dress that she's wearing , and if it's not new, then just tell her that it looks new on her because she livens up everything she wears. The question is, "if you say those things, are you lying?" Here's what makes it not a lie; if you develop yourself into a man who genuinely cares about the subtle changes that go on in a black woman's life, then it will never be a lie. When a black woman suddenly throws out the grandma drawers and starts wearing "T-back" bikini panties, it's because she wants you to notice; not because she just out of the blue acquired a taste for the feeling of string being up her butt.

To properly love the soul of a black woman you must first know your own soul. Think back to Newton's law again… Your soul must convey to you that it wants to gel with the soul of a black woman, closely followed by the mind and the heart on a common route to a single destination; then you are not unequally yoked." It's like being a judge in a wine tasting contest and you've never tasted any wine and sneaking a sip from your Father's glass during Thanksgiving dinner doesn't count.

Thanksgiving 2012, I know it's out of sequence, but try to keep up anyway. That was the first time I put my hands on her in an unpleasant way. There were an additional two times to follow but we'll address those later on. We decided to shop and cook together for our Thanksgiving meal.

Upon arrival at my apartment it was determined that she was to take on all of the domestic duties and I should sit in my recliner and relax until she was done; I concurred. In fact, I became so relaxed that I fell asleep and unbeknownst to me at the time, doing that actually made her feel very good. Several hours had passed, the aroma of good soul-food cooking was tickling my nostrils, all of the taste-testing was done and it was time to eat.

She prepared my plate right down to the dessert and big glass of pink lemonade and we commenced with prayer. "God, thank you for the food that we are about to receive and the blessings that you have bestowed upon us. Thank you for the wonderful heart of this beautiful woman that you have put in my life and thank you for yet another day of love, life and liberty. In your Holy name I pray. Amen."

Everything was great until I noticed a small portion of Squash on my plate. Before I could voice my objection she interjected and pleaded with me to just try it. I adamantly opposed it. Big mistake! Remember what I told you about the Eggs Extraordfamous? You see, it wasn't the idea that I didn't like Squash or even that she had eaten my eggs and shrimp without saying a word about not liking either of them.

The problem was that she put her heart into preparing that meal and I wasn't even willing to try the Squash. She hit the roof and proceeded to trash the entire meal. I made an attempt to stop her but she became more aggressive and demanded that I do not touch her. That's when it happened; I grabbed her by both arms and pinned her against the wall. It was only my intention to gain control and get her to snap out of her rage, but she didn't see it that way. All she knew was that I restrained her physically and that she saw it as abuse. For the record, I never struck her and never would.

Of course it ended up with us having sex on the coffee table to make things calm again, but it didn't make things righteous. **"Clearly I was wrong on both counts of not trying her dish and pinning her against the wall."** Unfortunately, there was nothing that I could say or do to take it back. Remember my quote?

Gentlemen, we have to learn to think about, anticipate and consider the consequences of our actions before we commit the act! Does that excuse the bad attitude? Of course not, but isn't prevention the preferred approach? I again reflect upon one of my spoken-word pieces, **"The most precious**

gift that God gave man is the ability to make a woman smile." Jb brown "Think Not; Thought Not. So ask yourself a question, "When are we the most motivated to make our women smile?" Is it in the morning, afternoon or night? Or is it when she's sad, lonely or depressed? What about on a holiday, birthday or a special occasion?

When striving to reach the soul of a black woman every effort to make her smile is a precious time. Don't get it twisted, everyone disagrees sometimes at various points in life, but it's how you handle those disagreements that make all the difference in the world.

I was told before that I have a way of telling people to go to hell and make them feel like I'm doing them a favor and that I could sell Satan a glass of ice-water. I don't think I ever want to test that theory but I did get the point. I'm blessed with that ability to make a woman smile, as with all men. The challenge is "using it."

"TENDER MOMENT"

What's the meaning of a tender moment?

Is it a soft kiss in the morning or a warm smile at night?

Is it a text in the middle of the day, just to convey, that

Baby I don't feel right about away the way that you left me

Cause you didn't say, "I love you," and I didn't say, "I love you more."

See I used to adore the way you'd laugh when I'd say something silly; And you'd say that I'm beautiful and I'd say, "Really?"

You see the way I deepened the voice? Just to let you know

That a man can be beautiful, and I'm not afraid to show my Tender Moment; But just for a moment; now bring it back.

Then we'd gaze at each other with this blank stare in our eyes

Like deer in the headlights when the cars drive by, then I'd cry; Oh yeah, I cry… A single tear falls from my eyes

You would wipe it, kiss your finger and say, "Baby, it'll be alright."

I know what she did to you; I know the way she made you feel

I would never do those things to you cause baby I keeps it real

And real good, if you know what I mean.

Martin Luther King Jr. said, "The ultimate measure of a man

Is not where he stands in times of comfort and convenience

But where he stands in times of challenge and controversy."

So does that mean that we can only see the good times?

Baby you're not Florida and I'm not James

We don't live in the ghetto and

I will never proclaim to be everything

Just everything to you

What's the meaning of a tender moment?

We always want to see the bright side and

We never want to see the rain

We stride to find the pleasure in life but

Baby sometimes pleasure can bring us pain

I just want to love you, and I promise you that right now

The greatest gift that God gave man

is the ability to make a woman smile

and now you know the meaning of a Tender Moment.

It's the moment when you look in my eyes and you realize

That "You are everything and everything is you."

And I'm everything that you want me to be. I'm done!

PARRISH THE THOUGHT

I don't want you to think that it was all bad. We had a few tender moments; there just weren't very many. Let's see if I can think of a few… My birthday, July 18th 2012, I was instructed to be dressed and waiting in the parking lot of my apartment at precisely 7:00 pm. All of my efforts to convince her to tell me who was picking me up failed, so I complied as I was requested and to my slight surprise a black stretch limousine arrived a few short moments after 7 to pick me up and whisk me away. I was disappointed to find that she was not inside; I felt lonely, but happy at the same time.

I called a few family members to share my joy as I pretended that I was some big shot going to a red carpet event. Along the way I fantasized about what I would do to her if she was in there with me. About a half hour later I arrived at my destination to her and a close friend of hers waiting for my entrance. Anticipation of the crowd grew more and more intense as I intentionally prolonged my exiting of the car.

Actually, I was just putting on my shirt, but they didn't need to know that. When I exited all eyes were on me. It was a great feeling and she stood proudly awaiting her prince charming to approach her with a welcome kiss; so I obliged her.

We made our way to the rear seating area where only a few loyal and humble people cared enough to show up. Despite the fact that the numbers in attendance was low Monee's demeanor never wavered from the joyful and happy soul that reflected excitement from the moment I stepped out of the limo. Her eyes gleamed, her teeth shined and she kissed me as if I had just returned home from a year tour in Iraq and she had been waiting patiently and faithfully the whole time. Gentlemen, in order to achieve the goal of loving the soul of a black woman there are some essential words and phrases that we just have to know; there's no getting around it.

I've talked about these things throughout the book so far; now I'm going to list them. Attention, affection, reciprocation, and yes sir, respect! My best friend says that he believes that I provoked Monee' to have most of the flare ups that she had to which I replied, "I agree," but only because to a large degree I believe that provocation is fueled by perception. If your lady says that she feels you have gained weight and you are too heavy on top of her now and you say to her, "You have lost your damn mind." Does that mean that you are calling her crazy? If she perceived it as such, then to her it may and that just might provoke her to respond in a very harsh way.

This one has, "What's the value" written all over it. Lesson VII, remember? What was the value of her telling you that you gained weight and are too heavy to be on top of her? What is a viable option? How about, "Baby, can we start walking together? I feel like we're both gaining weight and we can certainly use the exercise for our hearts." Pride probably won't let her say that, huh?; Especially if she is 5' 6" and weighs 128 pounds.

What about his response; could he have skipped the sarcasm? Of course! He could have come back with, "Okay, baby. Will you go to the gym with me? Maybe you can be out in front of me and if I catch you, I can have my way with you." See, the thing about it is that her comment is the lessor of the two evils. A woman can more often get away with expressing her true feelings than a man.

Not to mention the fact that you must consider the thought of her telling you versus allowing some other man to get her attention. The challenge with that is she could have perhaps been a bit less coarse; maybe leaving off the part about you being too heavy to be on top of her or she could have suggested going to the gym together. It seems that we just forget to conduct the interview process when seeking a mate. It's okay to "overlook" some things when you know that it's just a fly-by-night hook up or a one-night stand, but when you're searching for that soul-mate all things must be considered.

Women are inherently born with a nourishing nature about themselves but the black woman takes it as a personal mission, and if she doesn't accomplish her goal, she feels that she misrepresented all black women. They fall in love with a man's potential and spend countless time afterwards trying to "fix" him or change him into what she wants. The sad part is most of the time the black man's motivation is driven by the superficial aspects of what he sees and that fades, but the soul of a black woman never fades.

So let's look at it from the other perspective; the woman. What if you say to your woman that she appears to have gained some weight? Big mistake! What is a more subtle approach right out of the gate? Is there a subtle approach to talking to a woman about her weight?

The right approach is to be clear about your feelings during the interview process; you know, the thing that we seem to keep forgetting about. Let's "What's the value" this one. Humans are made up of 3 distinct parts; the body itself, the spiritual body and the soul, which is the mind. This is not to be confused with the brain, which is a weighted and measurable thing, but the mind does the processing and represents the soul.

Sorry to break it down to you folks, but "soul" has nothing to do with color, being "hip" or having "swagger." It also has absolutely nothing to do with a train. We tend to adopt words and use them enough to mean one thing until society accepts it.

Believe it or not, there's someone for everyone! Even the crazy people are eventually matched with someone else that's equally as crazy and they get along just fine. That's why when it's said that you have to treat her as you would yourself, it makes perfect sense. Let's take going out or to the bar for example; a man that doesn't like the bar life won't tolerate a woman that loves it. It's not that he doesn't understand it or even dislikes it.

It is not a part of his nature. Here's another example; A woman that is in her late 30's and doesn't have children would probably not last long being with a man who has children because if she doesn't have a medical condition that prevents her from having children, then she obviously didn't desire to have any.

She could have felt that children would interfere with her career path or maybe she felt that she wasn't cut out to be a parent. The key here, as with all aspects, is to determine that during the "interview period," and that's when you put yourselves on even ground. We become so afraid of losing or missing out that we completely ignore what our heart is truly telling us to do. You should always **"be sure that the depths of your soul match the surface of your existence."** Jb brown. Translation; set your standards and stick to them! This way you're never stepping beyond your means and you can master loving the soul of the woman that you choose.

Different women have different standards and requirements on how to love them, but trust me you can never love a black woman too much. Though it may not be said, your love for her is measured in everything that you do. If you don't believe me, eat the last chicken wing without offering it to her first and see if you don't hear about it! In a past marriage, we lived in a 4 bedroom house and I used one of the rooms as "my office" and I kept it locked. Big mistake! From my perspective I was shielding it from the kids and expressing my individuality. Newsflash, there is no "individuality" when you're in a marriage or relationship with a black woman.

Loving her soul means knowing that she wants to have an office too or perhaps just sharing yours would be enough since that means being together. It was an insult to her that

I didn't feel that her skills warranted having one. She also felt that I was hiding something and I was putting myself above her as well. Locks are made for honest people because if a crook wants in, he will get in and the power of her voice is all the lock that's needed to keep the children out.

The same Pastor that I mentioned earlier said in his counselling session that marriage is not 50/50 it's 100/100, which means when "we" bought that house together we both owned 100% of it and everything in it.

So what happens when one of you already owns a house? Well, that's when the man has to realize his mission. In the world of prenuptial agreements, alimony and "I'm gonna take you for everything you got!" We walk in fear and approach relationships with a world of caution. These things prohibit you from taking that concept into consideration, but if you exercised a little patience and good judgment, then you would discover the things you need to know during that interview period.

DISCUSSION QUESTION—HOW MUCH SAY SHOULD YOU HAVE IN HOW HE SPENDS MONEY?

CHAPTER VI

"LEARN HOW TO BALANCE IT ALL"

This is just the right time for me to say, "I'm not perfect." God had his Angels and I promise you that I wasn't one of them, nor am I a saint. It took many years for me to learn the things that I know about loving the soul of a black woman, but it's taken equally as many for me to accept it and learn to execute my knowledge. It's like alcoholism, the hardest part is admitting it, but once you take that first step everything falls right in place.

It becomes so natural that you won't even realize what's going on. What makes it so difficult is fighting against it. You have to ask yourself, "is it really that hard to be honest and treat her with respect?" If you can't, then don't get in the relationship; it's that simple! If you survey 100 black women, I guarantee that 80% of them will give you those two items as what they want from a man.

The truth is they want security; the attention and affection are part of what makes them feel secure. Go back and read again what I said about respect and what it really means to a black woman. If you like playing video games, hanging with the fellas, going to the clubs or any other activity that requires you spending time away from her, then you are fighting a losing battle.

It's not rocket science! It's simple, if you put ice in boiling water, then it's going to continuously melt, but if you put ice in standing hot water, then it's going to neutralize once the intensity of the ice meets or exceeds the intensity of the heat. Think about it; the point of which all things are equal is called balance.

Remember I said that I had a hard time trying to decide if I wanted to have sex, make love or just slam Monee'? The truth of the matter is you don't really make love to a woman's body. You make love to her mind! **"Once you learn how to make love to a black woman without touching her then you are delving into the deepest depths of her soul. Have you ever been having sex with a woman and she just started crying? I have… When you ask what's wrong, she says, "I just love you so much!" That's when you know you're making love to**

her soul and no amount of physical penetration can ever compare to it." jb brown

So how do you make love to a woman without touching her? Since true love-making is based on a oneness that comes from true love, then you have to explore and get to know the mind "soul" the same way that you explore and get to know her body. The same way that you learn her "G-spot," her sensitive areas and the way she responds to a certain touch is how you approach the soul. There is an attraction, stimulation, positive friction, secretion and an orgasmic level. Trust me, once you see it you will know and you won't have to question what it looks or feels like.

With all the physical mass in the human body, three types of muscles, and 206 bones there is only one G-Spot, therefore of all the millions of thoughts and mental desires you have to find her psychological G-Spot. The same thing applies to her mentally sensitive areas and take care and time to notice how she responds to things that you say.

The same way that she is aroused by your touch she will be aroused by your words, hence the positive friction. Her body will start to tingle; her eyes will gleam and focus only on you. She will hang on your every word, ergo, the erection and finally she will open up to you her deepest and darkest secrets, which is the orgasmic level. Her words will be unimaginably pure, her voice will be extremely clear and her connection to you will be stronger than any bond that you have ever felt before since the day you left your Mother's womb.

You can never stop dating… Let's reflect back upon Maya Angelou's thoughts about not forgetting the way people make you feel. Men have to be on a never ending cycle of regurgitating every thought, action and feeling that he does to make a woman smile or feel good. This of course emanates from the first "hello" and the first date.

This is the thing that drives the entire relationship but people seem to forget that so quickly. People say that an elephant never forgets. Well elephants must have taken lessons from women! Women not only remember everything, but they hold on to it and hold it against you.

So you want her to be understanding... Most women are, but it's the way that they respond to the many facets of life that throws you off balance. If you tell your lady that money's tight and you can't afford to engage in a certain activity, then you had better make damn sure that you don't engage in anything else that requires spending money.

Likewise, you had better not engage in anything with anyone else even if it doesn't take money. She understands that you may not have extra money all the time, but it doesn't always take money to give her time. For every video game, round of golf or hanging with the fellas is time taken away from her.

Think back to the very first time you asked her out on a date and she said yes. You get all of her info, clean up the car, get your hair cut, select just the right outfit and head out to her place to pick her up. You arrive right on time and perhaps even spring for some flowers. You open the doors, pull out the chair and allow her to order first. Her smile lights up the room and your confidence serves as the insulation that surrounds her every feeling. Fellas, you have to duplicate that and put it into circulation! Another newsflash; some women would have settled for you meeting her some place, showering, wearing clean clothes and paying for at least half of the bill.

When you do all the things as described previously it is a strong indication that you have a clue about reaching the soul of a black woman and that makes them feel good. Therefore, you have to continue to make her feel that way because she won't forget. I told you before that loving the soul of a black woman requires a lot of studying.

Let me give you something else to think about; a black woman constantly seeks her soul-mate, but she also wants her man to be her "soulmate". On the other hand, the male often seeks a soul-mate, but he seldom permits the woman to be his "sole" mate. How many times have you heard a woman say, "I don't ask for much"? She says that because **"Blessed is he who expects nothing for he shall never be disappointed."** Alexander Pope. Far too many women have settled for the idea that men are born to be unfaithful and are inherently prone to have more than one woman.

Ladies, if you believe that, and you truly want to live by that theory, then that's your prerogative. Joe said in his song, "I Wanna Know," I wanna know what makes you cry, so I can always be the one to make you smile. I love that concept! The problem with that is you have to be a really strong person to master it because you hold all the keys.

Most of us hide behind our emotions because we are afraid of getting hurt and we have trust issues derived from bad experiences in other relationships. Trust me, a woman remembers the specific feeling she gets every time she meets a guy that captivates her interest because she builds upon that feeling. It's not a new feeling for every guy.

Remember, women are driven by emotions and their emotions are always in order. When she is disrupted and becomes upset about something only her reactions are distorted; her emotions remain intact. A woman usually knows within the first 5 minutes if she's interested in a man and if she's sexually attracted to him within the first 15.

She meets a great guy; let's define a great guy. He's attractive, funny and nice but attraction is very subjective. Remember one man's trash… Funny, selective and nice is universal. So essentially only one of those 3 traits is a mutually sound attribute.

She likes his personality; the funny thing about that is I'm willing to bet that most people can't define the difference between personality traits or types. For example, type A personality folks are impatient and achievement-oriented, and are prone to coronary heart disease, while type B are easy-going, relaxed individuals who are apt to become alcoholics. How's this for a challenge? I'm type B but have never had a drink a day in my life. Type A through studies have also been discovered to develop personality disorders. A person can display traits of Extroversion or Introversion, which translates into attitude.

An extroverted person will display outward tendencies such as speaking loudly, involving themselves in conversations that has already gotten started but they will butt in and in many cases take over, they strive off of behavior, action, people, and things. Introverts, adversely, draw their energy from reflection and ideas.

They get charged up from thinking. There are 16 personality types and while I will only name, but not define them it opens the door to consider deeper thought when determining if you like or dislike someone's personality. There is the duty fulfiller, the mechanic, the nurturer, the artist, the protector, the idealist, the scientist, the thinker, the doer, the guardian, the performer, the caregiver, the inspirer, the giver, the visionary and finally the executive.

Once you determine what your own personality type is it will be much easier to seek out and find someone who will mate perfectly with you. I have often said that I want a female version of me because I love myself some me! There have been a few who initially opposed my position on that, but later came back to me with a different perspective.

It only makes sense; if you like it cold and dark in the house, then why would you want to be with someone who likes it bright and hot? If you are laid back, preserved and quiet, why would you want to be with someone that is loud, feisty and always on the move?

The first response is usually the same from all people; you need some differences or you will get bored. You balance each other. Let's talk about how stupid that is. How can you get bored with yourself? Anyone that does nothing 100% of the time does so by his own will and if he links up with someone who wants to go most of the time, then either he will be forced to stop going or the other will be forced to go. Either way, someone has to be removed from their contentment. Okay, let's get back on this great guy that was met.

He dresses nice, at least on that day, at that time, he appears to be clean, he has good moral values, a good outlook on life, he has a good job, nice car and family values. Most women appreciate a man with good family values, whether she has or wants children or not. So what's the missing element? How about the way that he treats you? You can't know that until you interact. Does he stimulate your mind?

Does he pay attention to the little things? Oh, wait a minute! What about the ring finger? Does he have two cell phones? Is he cautious about telling you where he works or giving you his home phone number or address? I guess I messed up that thought about your great guy, huh?

He's probably still a great guy but the point is all of those things have to be cleared up and established in the beginning. Skipping ahead causes those emotions to build without a strong foundation, then when a storm blows through it yields extensive damage. To love the soul of a black woman you have to be prepared for the storm before it comes. **"The time to prepare for war…"** I used to love the way Monee' would just smile so vigorously when I'd come around; it didn't matter what she was doing or where she was at, this great big beautiful and tender smile would drape her face and I would tingle.

Hebrews 4:12 says, **"For the words of God is living and active; Sharper than any double-edged sword. It penetrates even to divide soul and spirit, joints and marrow; it judges the thoughts and attitudes of the heart."** Many people equate body and soul to be one in the same, but Hebrews clearly nullifies that myth. Soul designates the feelings, wishes and will of humans. The black woman has taken so much care, time, patience and effort in getting to know herself and the key to man loving her soul is to surrender equal exertion to do the same. **"There is so much about one's self that is suppressed when not with the right person."** jb brown

Have you ever noticed that when a couple is really compatible how easy her life appears to be? Sustaining a relationship with problems that's not in tune is very hard work. The mental stress that's put on an unhappy woman from a bad relationship is equal to, if not greater than, that of a tough job. I'm not even talking about a physically abusive situation; the challenge comes from the high demand that the black woman puts on herself; not measuring up to those standards is what causes the issues.

Think about it; the desire is to be perfect in every way and in every aspect of all that she does; hence, the man not taking notice and showing appreciation of that is where the respect barrier comes in. Try this on for size; every black woman is born with the traits. When there's a black woman that doesn't display the traits we have the tendency to say she has poor values and low self-esteem, but nothing could be further from the truth. Actually she just compromised her standards to achieve "ownership."

Do you know anyone, ever known anyone or have you personally been engaged in an extra marital affair. A woman that cheats with a married man is often fulfilling her need for love and belonging, but no matter how good she's being treated she will surreptitiously leave that relationship if she's presented with a single man, even with much lower standards, worse characteristics, and not very good personality traits in order to achieve ownership.

A woman cannot lay legitimate claims on a married man; it's as simple as that. If she calls or text him to say she wants to see him and he replies disclosing that he and his wife are going to dinner and a play together, she can only be upset about it and keep it to herself. She can't go off on him about it.

With a single man that she has claimed ownership over, she can stand up and make some noise if he says that he is going to spend the evening out with another woman. I know it may sound crazy but think about it; I bet you probably know someone in that situation. Hell, you may be in one yourself! The black woman is so driven to have ownership that she doesn't even acknowledge the material things because it's being pitted against her morals and self-actualization.

I have often asked the question "Is there a difference between dating, seeing each other and being in a relationship?" What do you think? The responses have varied insomuch as "dating is when you're just trying to get to know each other and keeping your options open." "Seeing someone is when it's more serious and it's one on one." And "A relationship is more of a commitment." Personally, I'm confused about the interpretation between seeing someone and a relationship.

With me it's all the same; if I'm dating someone, then it's all about that person. I just don't get into the whole multiple dates or keeping the options open. Don't misunderstand me, I dated several girls at the same time many years ago but there are many lessons learned from that, which usually result in being alone and trust me, *"Reservations for One"* ain't no fun!

"RESERVATIONS 4 1"

Ain't no sunshine when she's gone; even a condemned man don't want to be alone.;

How can you have sunshine without the bright sunny rays?

It's like trying to have the summer without the bright sunny days.

The wind, the rain, the birds in the trees all seem to multiply by thousands when you live by yourself, eat by yourself, sleep… by yourself.

The days are long; the nights are cold,

Even your favorite TV show seems to drag on forever.

Every voice you hear; every face you see,

Is a constant reminder of what used to be.;

Knock, knock, knock… Ring, ring, ring… You don't want to answer cause it's just the same old thing.

All your thoughts of yesterday become the frustrations of today,

which somehow festers into the pain and sorrow of tomorrow…

All your dreams of the future are now the nightmares of the present, and you don't dare venture into the memories of the past.

Ain't no sunshine when she's gone.

One day seems like forever when you're living on your own.

Your emotions take over; it's impossible to conceal;

You're supposed to love the way that love makes you feel.

The toughest part is facing your heart and accepting the reality

That although you're shopping for two, cooking for two, preparing for two;

The only one that's eating is you… You think back to what you used to do; You regret all those times you didn't try to hide when that ghetto booty walked by and you would break your neck to look too; ooh!

Only now when you turn back there's no one there but you... It ain't no fun, Reservations for One;

Yeah, it's tough living all alone, but like my man Bill said, "Ain't No Sunshine When She's Gone!"

jbstar 2011

I was extremely lonely before I met Monee'. I remember going to a local bar one night and presented my name to the hostess for seating. She asked me if I was alone and I jokingly replied, "Yep, just like the lady on the TV show, Frazer." She laughed and told me that she would spare me the embarrassment of announcing that over the Public Address system.

It became an ongoing joke between the two of us as I continued to come in weekly for my "all you can eat" crab-legs Friday. I hate being single! The first time I went to the movies alone I sat in the parking lot an hour and a half horrified at going in alone. I watched others go in and come out all coupled up. I finally left but returned the next night to conquer my fear.

I went on to watch an astonishing 17 movies by myself. I became a pro, though I still didn't like it. Being alone is just not my cup of tea and it's sad that it's taken me this long and this many relationships to finally put the proper value on a relationship. Please know that I take full responsibility for my part in every relationship that went south.

It's sad though that all of my breakups were caused by my overwhelming dedication to work and not due to infidelity.

I have been accused of cheating with my work, though. I guess you're wondering if I'm going to give it up. I said that I have, but here I sit writing this book or does this count?

Bubba Sparxxx said, "I ain't choose to rhyme; rhyming chose me…" That's the way I feel about writing, acting and directing. It comes so easy to me that I know it is what I was put on this earth to do and I'm good at it. I see and hear of others struggling with writer's block and getting into character. I've never experienced that through 14 scripts, two books, over 100 spoken-word pieces and 30 videos.

That's why I know without an ounce of doubt that's what God intended for me to do. I guess I still didn't really answer the question. I want very badly to be in a committed relationship, whereas she accepts and supports my business endeavors, but more importantly I need to learn how to include, respect, love, honor her and balance the whole thing so that we both remain happy.

DISCUSSION QUESTION—WHAT CONSTITUTES CHEATING?

CHAPTER VII

"DON'T LET THE OUTSIDE IN"

You all will probably think that because I told you the story about us and Veronica that this chapter may seem a bit contradicting. Well, I'm about to share a whole lot more about some sexual escapades and situations that also should have never happened. Let's start off with a situation that took place on Father's day. Monee' decided to surprise me by treating me to the zoo. As with all her other planned events it was meant to be somewhat elaborate.

She phoned and asked if I would mind entertaining the thought of hanging out with some of her relatives at the zoo and I graciously accepted her invitation. She shut down early for the day and came to pick me up. She said that we were going to chill with her relatives for a few, but the night belonged to us.

LESSON 7. "WHAT'S THE VALUE?"

When we arrived at the zoo we both intentionally left our cell phones behind in the car so we could focus on each other and use the time for bonding. We walked hand in hand and had a great conversation. It took me a minute to catch on that her relatives were the animals. I made so many wrong choices on that day until I damn near wish that I had stayed home.

As soon as we hit the gate I messed up. Trying to be cheap, I didn't know that Father's got in free that day, so I walked in and left her at the gate. Wrong choice # 1. She was trying to call me back for a part of the presentational surprise, but I insisted on remaining inside; she looked past it and we went on inside.

We walked around slowly and discussed each animal in detail as we read the literature and shared some special moments. We spent quite a bit of time in the snake pit, which is my favorite area and she was much obliged to hang on to my arm and I loved every minute of it. The time to close was drawing near and there was still much to see.

She reassured me that we could return on another day to view the rest if I was dissatisfied with our incomplete visit, and we made our way towards the exit. At the front entrance there was a welcome area with bathrooms and souvenir stores. A female wearing some extremely short shorts, a tight-fitting shirt and some flats on, was walking around and I disrespectfully did everything I could to sneak a peek. Wrong choice # 2 of the day!

Michael Baisden had a segment on his show one day called, "Is it okay to look." I asked several women that question, to which they all individually and separately replied, "That's what God gave us eyes for, to look. As long as he's not bent all over breaking his neck, I think it's okay." Some added, "It's just looking.

I don't see anything wrong with it." Each time I would smile slightly and respond, "Let's say you're having a bad day; your hair wouldn't do right, your car wouldn't start, somebody cut you off on the road and your boss is on your ass about a project he wants completed two days earlier than originally requested. You call up your boyfriend or husband and meet for lunch and you begin to vent.

Suddenly a female with a nice ass, wearing a tight-fitting dress and some pumps walks by and right in the middle of your story he turns his head to look at her ass; tell me it's okay then! Monee' took time from her day to come pick me up to take me out for Father's day and I was totally out of line for looking at that female.

She worked 12-14 hours a day on the weekend and I worked Monday through Friday during the day. I had plenty of time to look at other women, but my selfish ass couldn't resist sneaking a look. The sad part about it was the fact that she overlooked it. She knew I was looking but she still pretended that it was all good.

We both completed our visits to the bathroom and then went into the store together. We admired a lot of the items but didn't make a purchase. We left and decided to take a more scenic route back to the car via the picnic area.

As we were nearing the end of the park we spotted a group of people cooking bar-b-que and having a good time, they gestured for us to come over and we walked over to say hello. Immediately we felt a connection, they offered for us to join them and we accepted. Wrong choice # 3! We both got plates and began to introduce ourselves, but individually… Wrong choice # 4.

Shortly after consuming the first piece of chicken I made wrong choice # 5 and 6. I walked over to the car to check the messages on my phone and left her there to socialize with them. Of course the vultures swooped in for the kill. Shortly after returning from the car I had to use the bathroom, so once again I placed yet another wedge between us by leaving her alone again. I was gone for at least 20 minutes, including the 150 yard walk to the restroom and back.

She had planned for us to spend the evening together bonding and I screwed it up by leaving her several times. Well that's not all; we stupidly agreed to go to their house for an after party. On the way for some reason or another we went at it again. She was furious and let me have it up one side and down the other.

I was completely oblivious at the time; once again hind site… It seemed as though I broke every one of my own rules about sticking together. I failed to establish and maintain the united front. Fellas, there should never be any doubt as to who your woman is to you and you are to her.

Fellas, I'm not saying that each time other people are around you have to announce out loud that she is your lady or wife, but people can determine it based on your body-language. When you leave your Mother's bosoms and your Father's arms you have to create a united front with your mate. This bond wreaks strength and shows others that to speak ill of either of you is to speak ill of both of you! To offend her is to offend me; I am her and she is me.

There must never be fear of repercussions from others knowing "up front" that you will share every word and all info spoken to, around or in front of you, especially if it's about her or you!

Ladies, when striving to achieve the destiny of your man loving your soul you can't be concerned with what others think and let no one control or determine what you talk to your mate about when your heads are laying on those pillows on "your" bed! Several things were kept from me by Monee' that were said behind my back because of fear that I would say something to those who spoke ill of me.

The world should know that the two of you are together because this strengthens the bond even more. You will never know how strong the walls are until they come up against strong winds. Ruth had told me several times before we were married that she was curious about being with women. For the first six months I blew it off and chalked it up to her trying to trap me, however no matter what was said or done, she maintained her position that she wanted to try it.

I had grown pretty sick of hearing it so I figured it was time for her to put up or shut up. She went on travel one month to visit her Mother and the opportunity presented itself. I met Chrissy, Hispanic, 5' 5" tall, 116 pounds, long dark hair and the sweetest accent you would ever want to hear. Just the tone of her skin alone made me tingle all over and want her all the more. I can't remember a time being more attracted to a female.

I met her at the drug store and noticed that she appeared to be feeling a bit down, so I cautiously engaged in idle conversation with her so as not to come across too aggressive. Immediately she began to confide in me and disclosed that her man treated her like shit. Of course that was a roadmap to me that led directly into her arms.

She despised him and at that moment I was looking really good to her. Obviously I was thinking a bit selfishly, although Ruth had already confessed her feelings about bumping coochies with a woman, therefore I figured I should be direct and upfront with Chrissy about my true intent. FYI, I wanted to sex her so bad that my mouth watered.

With Ruth gone for two more days I was free to work on Chrissy and get her primed up. She was down for it, so all that was left then was to call Ruth's bluff to see what she was holding. The day of her return finally came and the plot began.

At the time I owned a high-top customized van with a hideaway bed in the back, so I had Ruth hideaway on it while Chrissy and I went for a ride up front. Ruth listened closely as Chrissy and I discussed the idea of having a threesome to confirm her interest. Once Ruth heard everything she needed it was time to reveal her presence to Chrissy.

They both acted surprised though I knew they were fully aware of each other being there. The two of them were instantly connected to each other. We went back to our apartment and it was left up to me to initiate the action; they both put on this BS shy routine, so I loosened things up by giving them my own rendition of a private dance as I slowly and methodically stripped away each article of clothing to the mesmerizing sounds of Teddy Pendergrass', "Turn of the Lights." After I got them both nice and hot I suggested we move the party to the bedroom.

I wasted no time making love to both of them. We alternated grinding, smacking, and slapping like a pendulum, me to Ruth, Ruth to Chrissy and Chrissy right back to me! The action continued as our shadows faded into the night and we became one, only to be torn apart by the eruption of three physical beings spewing their body fluids all over each other. To my surprise, as told by Ruth weeks later, she was not satisfied; she wanted more and I must confess so did I. The three of us got together a few days later to embellish our new found connection. We took the van to the drive-in movies and we stretched out on the back bed with me in the middle. Oh my God! What have I done to deserve this?

Right at the end of the film I made my move on Chrissy. I began with a few subtle touches to her waistline, lower back and ass cheeks, but she squirmed and rejected me as if we had never been together before; I was a bit bewildered but not discouraged. Finally, she responded verbally, "stop, jb." "What's the problem?"

I asked innocently as Ruth sat up and took notice, then intervened. "It's okay, Chrissy, I don't mind." She comforted her with a reassuring tone and caressed Chrissy softly on her shoulder. Just as I began my second attempt to feel her up and she had given in, the attendant came around tapping on the window.

Furious about the mood being spoiled, I hurriedly scrambled to the driver's seat and drove off to find a place where we could park and continue. Unfortunately there was no destination close enough because as I drove away from the theatre Chrissy and Ruth began to drive on each other.

Their bodies meshed together like a bowl of mash potatoes and they were on pause by the simultaneous climax that left them both trembling on the back seat and me damn near wrecking the van trying to watch. I found a spot, stopped and practically begged them to do it again, but their reenactment just didn't have the same zest.

We went on to amass some 8-12 more adventures through the next few years. It had become second nature to us, but not realizing that the outside had completely invaded the inside. Each time a bigger wedge was driven between us and our raging lust caused us to do the wrong thing. There was Nadine from Food Depot, Kendra from the local college, Sabrina from the Family dollar store, Karin, Lexus and Furious from a strip club, Melissa from a night club and Loraine that we met through our Pastor. I don't even remember the other four but each one was just as exciting as the first. Although we were constantly exposed to several females in the business, I aspired to keep our tainted sex life separate.

One morning I scheduled a project out of town and put the responsibility of transportation upon myself. Unfortunately my car wasn't big enough to carry us all, so I enlisted the aid of Ruth to drive her vehicle and take half the people. As I was designating who would ride with whom I merely said to 3 people that "you 3 will ride with Ruth." She was furious! She felt so hurt as if I was just implying that she was only a driver and was nothing more to me. Once again I drove the wedges deep, letting the outside in, but wait, it ain't over yet.

I never said it would be easy! You have to develop a mental sense of awareness and not allow your environment to overcome you. We are prone to consistency, which means we are creatures of habit. Whenever we fall into a comfort zone that's what we grow to be used to. Let's take an "exotic dancer" for example; the average stripper will tell you that she's doing it only to work through college to get her degree, then you see her three or four years later and she is still right there stripping.

Or how many times have you ever talked to a stripper and her thoughts were "I'm just doing this until I can find something better?" Can you imagine how many hundreds of thousands of people who are degreed but working in something completely different? Hell, I know a lady who has a masters degree in clinical counseling but she's an administrative assistant, and probably smarter than most of the people that she works for. If you are blessed to work in the same field as your degree, rejoice!

Anyway, it took me a lot of years to "learn" to be faithful again. Part of the Lord's Prayer says "**lead us not into temptation**" but the flesh can definitely be tempting sometimes. Let me tell you about a situation I had with a stripper; believe it or not I was a very faithful man before I got a taste of the wild life. I recall the first time I cheated; I thought the world was gonna come to an end! I never prayed so hard in my life!

I just knew that God was going to strike me down at any moment but I'm remiss to say that with the aid of my best friend I soon got over it. So, let's get back on track; here's the story about the stripper I was about to share with you. One night I tipped out to a strip club and it was Ruth's birthday. She and I had gotten into it for something and she was angry with me. I met a stripper, Ecstasy, who agreed to come home with me as a surprise birthday gift for Ruth. Oh, I don't think I mentioned that Ruth is gay. Of course I didn't know it when we first hooked up.

She threw plenty of hints and in some cases told me straight up that she was "curious" about being with women. Ecstasy and I went in and I made the initial approach in an attempt to smooth out the situation and prepare Ruth. She was asleep and still a bit upset, so I broke it to her gently. I gave Ruth a few moments to compose herself then brought Ecstasy into our bedroom and made the introduction. It was an instant attraction between the two of them and they wasted no time showing it. Immediately they made physical contact and I watched eagerly as it slowly escalated into an all-out exploration of each other's body. They agreed upon my request to take a shower together and even allowed me to video tape it to commemorate the night that would not be soon forgotten.

Armed with my video camera and a stone stiff erection, I excitedly assisted both of them with disrobing and cordially guided them to the bathtub where sheer delight was about to make its way into their psyche. I recorded every angle that the space allowed; they caressed and massaged each other slowly and affectionately. As the passion increased the anticipation intensified. I continued to video as they completed their cleansing and toweling each other off. They made their way to the bed and I followed closely. They entered the bed and unrestricted actions took over the room.

I watched eagerly as they grind, kissed and caressed each other from head to toe, stopping momentarily in various places to explore the contours more closely and intimately. After several moments of passionate pleasuring to each other it was time for me to join the party. I began with some subtle touches to both of them and they responded in-kind. I made my way between the two of them and enthusiastically guided my pulsating penis to thrust its way into Ecstasy's warm, wet and well-kept vagina. Simultaneously, we both realized that I was flying without a cape, but it felt so delightful that several strokes elapsed before she curled up into the fetal position thereby terminating our union as the pounding sensation in my chest dissolved into a faint low thump.

It was a deadly game of Russian roulette and those few thrusts were well worth the risk. "You need to put on a hat!" she whispered softly as my body quivered from anxiety and the anticipation of busting an eruption inside her. Ruth and I were married and monogamous so we didn't readily keep condoms in the house, therefore I could only reluctantly retract and reply "Crap! I don't think I have one." Then you're going to have to just watch and keep on taping because I can't let you get up in me without one." She proclaimed with a hint of disappointment in her voice. The two of them reengaged in their tantalizing grinding session as I scrambled around desperately in search of protection.

I wanted that girl so badly that it produced a throbbing pain in the pit of my stomach. Finally I surrendered to temptation and eagerly rejoined the excitement in hope that she wouldn't notice my raw, unsealed nature. I was able to finagle my way back between Ecstasy's legs and managed to slip my hardened beef-stick inside her once again. Although sheer satisfaction was verified by the intense biting of her bottom lip combined with the harmonious sound of her passionate moans, she managed after a few more vigorous thrusts to realize that my search yielded a negative result.

The battle was lost but the war was still well in hand. Accepting that reentry would be denied, I adjourned to the edge of the bed and fulfilled my mission with a few light whacks. The feeling with "Mary Palmer" was nowhere near a comparison to Ecstasy's soft, wet tunnel, but the effort gave me the same end result. I continued to watch as they remained indulged in their licking, kissing and groping of each other's anatomy. It seemed like the right thing to do at the time. We… "I" just couldn't keep the outside out. Though Ruth and my relationship lasted some seven years, it hinged on the idea of us catering to the bisexual appetite that she had developed over the years.

We even tried to actually form a "tri-couple" relationship with Loraine. She was beautiful! She was tall, thin, very shapely, toned, with real hair and good teeth. That was the first time we made a public announcement professing our relationship. It started out nicely but quickly migrated into complete turmoil. We traveled and attempted to do everything together, but one of the primary issues was Loraine didn't like wearing clothes very much. She dressed very provocatively and it drew an enormous amount of undue attention to us. One night the three of us went to a local club and I was the envy of the spot. Imagine entering a crowded lounge with two beautiful women, one on each arm and I'm not even a celebrity.

We sat in the dignified area and gained privy of a direct path to the isolated dance floor. Loraine had a bit of the wild side in her system, so upon an eager but innocent gesture from a free spirited Caucasian chick she hit the dance floor wide open. As the thumping sound of the amplified music permeated our brains Loraine's firm and uncontained left breast found its way outside of her shirt on total display for all eyes to see. Of course she looked sexy as hell but I rather enjoyed the privilege of knowing that Ruth and I were the only ones who got to view and suck those babies, so I wanted it tucked away.

She was dancing so hard that she didn't even notice; I began to yell out to her, "Baby! Look down! Baby!" Her female dance partner noticed me gesturing to her and suddenly realized what I was saying. She got Loraine's attention by tapping her on her arm; Loraine looked down and riddled with embarrassment aggressively tucked her titt back in her shirt and briskly left the floor. "I'm done! That's enough for me," she proclaimed as she rejoined us at the table. We laughed a little as she found comfort in cuddling next to me on the right side as Ruth held claim to her position on the left. We finished our drinks and left shortly after that.

That was the third time that we had tried the tri-couple relationship and couldn't seem to make it work. Loraine and Ruth discovered a common love between them for "Mary Jane." I had no interest in recreational drugs so I didn't fit in where that activity was concerned. At first they would partake out on the porch but the cold weather quickly deterred them from that ambition. Then it became an issue of, "this is our home too! We shouldn't have to go outside to smoke." So they started going to Loraine's home, which meant spending many hours away from me and that just didn't work. After that, came the two of them taking trips together without me; that only opened up the can of worms even more. They were spending mad time together and I was left holding my balls. The agreement that Ruth and I made was that there would always have to be mutual attraction amongst all three of us and equal time spent but when I started complaining she gave me the speech about needing "girl time," and how in the hell does any man compete with that?

The truth of the matter was we should have never engaged in that outside activity to begin with. Sure it was fun and nice and even exciting, but when venturing to love the soul of a black woman it must be realized that "forsaking all others" and keeping them out is a major component of the mission. The black woman doesn't like being second to anything or anyone. Of course she understands that God will always come first, but since he is not here in the physical sense he gets a freebee. I developed a complex when I was growing up because my Mother used to always ask me, "Where are you going?" It used to drive me up the wall! "Who are you going to be with? What time are you coming back?" There were times when I would just cancel the whole trip because I didn't want to give her an answer. Well, that trait carried over to the ongoing generations. To know and monitor your every move ties a woman's worth directly to her feeling that nothing or no one else is more important. Think about it; they leave it to you to assume that it's out of concern or that they just want to know where you are in case something happens. Ha! That may have been a good sales pitch 30 years ago, but with technology today, it doesn't stand a chance.

Every time a man leaves a woman, in her mind, it's taking away from moments that she can have with him. The sad part about it is most women won't admit it, but they all feel the same way. It doesn't matter if he's going to the store, a game, the office, the club, a buddy's house or even a relative's house, you're still putting the outside before her.

DISCUSSION QUESTION—HOW DO "YOU" DEFINE COMPROMISE?

CHAPTER VIII

"LOVE BEFORE YOU LOVE"

Just one more try… Those four words had become the most familiar and favorite phrase to me in the English language. You know how you go through so many negative occurrences in relationships and every time you meet the next one you hope for a combination of all the good things from each one to be extracted and blended together to make the present? Well, Monee' was the exact opposite! She was a combination of all the bad things put together and rolled up into one and I was motivated by the thought that I could make it work. I felt her wrath within the first month that we were together but I didn't walk away when I had the chance.

Every time I said we were done she cried and begged and each time I responded in-kind. It was such a common response that it became second nature to me. We often speak of what we want in a mate, but the difference between what we want and what we are willing to do to get what we want are worlds apart, however the first step is always going to be knowing for certain what it is we want. See I know now that we both had serious issues with loving ourselves. Yeah we both often bragged about having two degrees and other certifications, but none of that is really important when it comes to true love. The best love affair I've ever had was with myself! I love myself some me!

Loving yourself begins with defining who you are, and the things that you do identify your character. We each must have an outlet; you are reading my outlet. I write, as illustrated in the next spoken word piece that I'm about to share with you. While out doing chores one day I spotted a lady that I found to be attractive. Actually she wasn't exactly my type but I chose to approach her anyway. I didn't stand a chance! She lit in on me like I was an Iraqi citizen, straight getting ready to blow some stuff up.

I WRITE, MY SISTAS, I WRITE

She was born, born in the summertime, thought she was grown by the spring;

Had 3 babies by 3 different men and still didn't learn a damn thing;

She has a hole in her lip and a ring through her tongue;

Gave a man every dime she had cause she thought she had him sprung. (Make sense of that)

And now, now your heart is so distraught that a man is a distraction;

But a real man completes his woman and supports her every action;

Sitting around crying about the things that you don't have;

Dropping it on your girlfriends and when you leave they laugh; (Oh yeah, they laugh)

Feeling sorry for yourself cause you have a G.E.D;

Now your so-called friends have turned, you turn to G.O.D

See, strength comes in numbers my sista, divided we will crumble;

God will always know your heart, you just gotta stay humble;

Every time that things get hard you feel there's nothing else;

Sista girl, take it from me, start with loving yourself;

See, I, I just wanna show you how foolish we've become;

You, you think because I say "hello" I'm just trying to get some;

But wait, until you know my true ambition, you should trust your intuition;

With no surprises, my honesty rises, you'll find I'm in submission;

And then, then before you pass me by, embrace your heart cause it won't lie;

And trust, not to say my words are true, but in the intellect God gave you;

And boo, turn around if it's not right, darkness is always revealed by light;

I write, my sistas… I speak through poetry taken from the heart;

We'll never reach the finish unless we reach a start;

I write, my sistas…

I write these words not to reap the reward;

I may live by the pen but I'll die by the sword.

I Write, My Sistas, I Write… I'm done!

jbstar 2011

When it comes to loving yourself it's sad that we seldom even think about the health risks that are involved with spreading ourselves too thin. Let's skip the obvious for a minute and talk about stress. Do you know that stress kills? Lying is very stressful; it will never cease to amaze me how so much effort has to go into keeping a lie going. Have you ever wondered what it would be like if you are 100% honest with your mate about everything all the time? Is that even possible? You would have to live a life that is completely sheltered and every step has to be calculated to a science.

If you get off from work early and decide to stop at the local strip bar for a quick drink and a couple of lap-dances, then when she calls and ask you "What did you do after work, baby?" If you reply, "Nothing," you have just perpetrated a lie that may have to be prolonged and covered to the end and that causes stress. The question becomes "what if you told her the truth?" Take it from me, the best approach is just not to go at all. Remember the "Is it okay to look" question? The bottom line is if you're not ready to give up the strip clubs, then just stay single because I promise you that she doesn't mean it when she says it's okay.

Stress also causes headaches, gray hair, aging and other major health issues. Loving the soul of a black woman requires you to allow nature to take its course in the most refine way humanly possible. That is not forcing anything and putting her first no matter what! I realize that it's a steep commitment but for so long we have settled for less. That's not to say that marriages and relationships haven't worked the way they are, but we're talking about taking it to another level; some modern day Romeo and Juliette type of stuff.

Now let's talk about the obvious fear of creeping and lying. By show of hands, how many of you say the words, "I love you," at least once a day? I mean, when you leave home, finish a conversation on the phone, or close a letter? I say "I love you" at least six times a day… to "me!" I love myself some, "me!" I got mirrors all over the house and where I don't have one you can be sure that there's something that casts a reflection. I guarantee I love myself some "me!" You see, I can't expect anyone to love and care for me if I don't love and care for myself.

Don't get me wrong; Fellas, I know you spend mad time in the Barber's chair getting that line tight and keeping that dome fresh. I know you stay iced up with all the latest jewelry and keep your gear pressed up and your kicks clean. And Ladies, you keep your nails "did," your hair tight, and I know you're always shopping for the nicest and cutest outfits to look good. But guess what!

Everything that looks good, ain't always good for you! How many people have ever smelled a rotten egg? Have you ever noticed that you don't really smell it until you break the shell? Check it out for yourself; take an egg and place it in a condition that will provoke it to spoil, then pick it up, look at it and smell it. Play with it a little, then crack it.

See if what you smell when you crack it is as pleasant as before you do. A.I.D.S. eats away at you from the inside out. You can bathe, put on deodorant, wear clean cloth, spray on cologne or perfume and none of that will fight the effects of A.I.D.S. It knows no names; it knows no age; it sees no faces; it doesn't smell cologne or perfume; it doesn't see nice clothes, shoes, jewelry… nothing! You have got to love yourself some "you!" You've got to say it every day! "I love myself some me!" Let's break down the acronym, Acquired, Immune Deficiency Syndrome. What's the key word? **<u>"Acquired."</u>** That means you got to get it.

That means it's something that has to infiltrate your body. It's not just something that we're predetermined to be born with. It's not a natural thing. So what does that say to me? That says I have to do something or something has to be done in order for this deadly disease to get inside my body. It doesn't just come along. The sad part about it is that there are so many misconceptions about how you get it and where it came from. Years ago I used to hear things like it came from Africa and Monkeys brought it into the U.S.

I used to hear that only homosexuals contracted and passed along the virus. I used to hear that prostitutes had it. I used to hear that you could only get it from having sex. You need to know that it didn't come from Monkeys. In fact, no one really knows where it came from, but what is important is how to prevent it. A.I.D.S. is a virus that is the end result of H.I.V. Human Immunodefeciency Virus. You don't just get A.I.D.S. Your body has an immune system that naturally fights off viruses, infections and foreign bodies. What the A.I.D.S. virus does is eats away at that immune system until you no longer have any natural defenses.

Once this happens, the medications no longer have any internal allies to stop your body from being destroyed by any and every form of bacteria, virus and disease that humans are subjected to. A.I.D.S gets into your bloodstream and attacks the body. You can't get A.I.D.S from kissing. You can't get it from touching someone who has the virus.

You can't get it from just getting their blood on yourself; however if that blood somehow enters your bloodstream from an open sore, by needle or absorption, then it could infect you. The only 100% way to avoid contraction is to live in a bubble, but since that's not practical, then preventive measures such as abstinence, infectious control practice, personal hygiene, awareness and just plain common sense certainly heightens the probability of avoidance.

I'd like for you to take a few moments to research some facts about A.I.D.S. and I don't want you to just read the stats; I'd like for you to imagine yourself as one of the numbers. I'd like for you to imagine that you are one of the victims and that your days are numbered and there's absolutely nothing that you can do about it!

When you're finished, I'd like for you to then think about all of the things that you can do now to prevent it. Loving the soul of a black woman necessitates the anticipation of considering every single aspect of what you can and should do to prevent her from feeling even an ounce of negativity.

Right now I partition the principals and leaders of all organizations to procure full length mirrors to be placed strategically throughout the school; on doors, walls, lunchrooms and all entrances so that every time someone enter a school, eat lunch, walk the halls or sit in a classroom, they glance in one of mirrors and say, "I love you!" I want you to say it right now, repeat three times; "I Love Myself Some Me!" "I Love Myself Some Me!" "I Love Myself Some Me!"

Loving yourself can cloud your judgment sometimes; without even realizing it you can seek attention through confirmation from another person and be giving up intimacy. When asked, "What is intimacy?" many people responds with some kind of sexual connotation, however there are so many things that we engage in day to day that has nothing to do with sex. For example, if a person is feeling down about the death of a loved one or something more simple like a pet and a coworker of the opposite sex seeks to comfort the individual, their response is an intimate moment.

There are only two things in this world that we truly own; that's your word and your thoughts. Allowing someone to share your inner feelings about the remorse of the demise of someone or something close makes them privy to an inner layer that everyone shouldn't have the privilege of experiencing. Let's say you're having problems at home with your significant other and you appear sad at work. You have just made yourself vulnerable to exposing your deep thoughts and becoming subject to rendering intimacy to someone else; sounds strange doesn't it? Think about it!

A woman that is striving to be with a man that loves her soul will yearn for the constant and deep conversation that comes with protecting himself from outside sources so that her man is giving it all to her. You can't even share your thoughts and feelings with your local bartender when you're striving to love the soul of a black woman because it takes away from the sincerity that comes from the first time being told. Ladies, don't think that you don't play a part in this too…

Most men are extremely reluctant to open up to his lady and pour out his emotions, and don't even think about seeing him cry, so the worst thing that you can do is ignore him or complain that he's talking too much. Never say that he's whining because you will only get one chance to put him down and that's exactly how he will take it.

Let me take you back to my childhood for a minute. I have five sisters and I grew up close with them. I learned early the benefits of appreciating the sensitivity level of the black woman. One would think that having the privilege of witnessing first-hand the things they went through with guys but doing the right thing is a choice, not so much a matter of knowing better. My Mother was very strict when it came to my sisters dating and much easier on the boys, which I never understood because it takes boys to date girls.

When they did get to date and a boy was allowed to come over, a big pillow was placed between them to keep them apart as they sat on the sofa in the living-room. I have witnessed many arguments and harsh discussions between my sisters and their boyfriends through the years. I watched and studied them like a college course. My main purpose was to learn everything I could about loving a black woman the right way. Unfortunately I picked up the good right along with the bad and that included teaching me to develop a "sharp tongue" as they said in the old days, and that led me to a near tragic incident in my manhood.

Lauren, 5' 4", 122 pounds, bright complexion, real hair, nice butt and a great smile; starting to notice a pattern? We met in Wal-Mart; what a great place to meet women! We met on the furniture aisle next to the computer desks. I watched her for a moment to ensure she was alone, and then I made my move. She went for it and we went on to develop a wonderful union with terrific rewards. She was so sweet, loving, patient, understanding and totally into me! I had found my paradise. We shared everything from time to love and laughter.

We were almost inseparable. Little did I know that there was a raging demon dwelling deep within her that would lead to fury like I had never seen in 8 years of military training and 4 years as an armed security police officer. One hot summer day I came home from work and my car air conditioner wasn't working, so needless to say my clothes became drenched from sweat and I had an event to go to later that evening. Tension between us was a bit elevated due to her rejection of my request to rub bellies the previous night, so our communication wasn't at its best.

I walked in and decided to grab a quick bite to eat before heading out. Lauren was still huffing and puffing from whatever she was pissed about the night before, so I just went about my way getting myself together. As I was about to take a shower to clean myself up a bit from all the sweat, she angrily approached me and demanded to know why I was taking a shower. "Are you f**king around on me?!" She asked with a coarse tone of voice to which I sarcastically replied, **"If you had done your duty last night, you wouldn't have to be worried about that!"**

Oh my God! All hell broke loose. "I'll show you, Motherf**ker!" as she walked hurriedly out of the room. Unaware of her intentions, I proceeded to the bathroom to get in the shower. The next thing I knew I felt a hand abrasively grab my right shoulder and I'm yanked around and pushed against the wall with my loaded and cocked 357 Magnum handgun pointed at my head.

"I told you Motherf**ker, you're not gonna cheat on me," she yelled angrily as the gun alternated between my head and my chest. "Lauren, put the gun down and stop trippin'." "Naw! You want to f**k around, I'll show you who you're f**kin' with!"

"I told you I don't play that!" she continued to scream and maintained her firm grip on the gun. Amazingly, I maintained my composure and pleaded with her once again, "Lauren, put the gun down and go relax, please." "I'll kill your Motherf**kin' ass! Awwww!" She yelled out as she finally dropped the gun and hurried out.

Wrong choice! Just that simple reply caused the situation to elevate to greater heights than I ever imagined. That pride factor kicked in and I made a bad choice. I could have avoided that blow up just by choosing to say, "Baby, the air conditioner is broken in the truck and I sweated on the drive home. I haven't cheated on you."

The point I'm making is you can't allow yourself to get caught up in the pride of the "snap back" syndrome to get the best of you. Loving the soul of a black woman sometimes mean pampering and catering to her most sensitive needs. You will find that every woman will get upset about something at some time in life. The degree of her display will vary from person to person and situation to situation.

I know people believe that perfect relationships don't exist and this book is dabbling into the implication that I am fantasizing about creating just that. However, what makes anything perfect? Perfect is defined as having all the required or desirable elements, qualities, or characteristics; as good as it is possible to be.

With that in mind we have to consider that most of the time we create our own negativity. For example, one day one of my partners, Jeff, came up on the scene where Monee' and I were talking at her business. Immediately I could sense her attraction to him.

Jeff is a personal trainer, who trains only women; Monee' had been recently working out with another trainer, but she constantly complained that he was unattractive, though very effective in his methods because they were somewhat strenuous. She expressed to me her thoughts of Jeff having "swag" and it would be her choice to have him train her. Wrong choice # 1, however upon her request, I gave her Jeff's number. Wrong choice # 2, then she asked me if I had a problem with him training her, to which I said yes I did have a problem with it.

At that time I had no idea that she had already made an appointment with him to do an assessment on her. Wrong choice # 3. Of course she asked me what was the problem and I told her I felt it was inappropriate; it could cause tension between Jeff and me; it would make me uncomfortable and was not worth the risk. Atlanta is saturated with personal trainers of both male and female so it wasn't necessary to use Jeff. Bearing in mind that I could have avoided the whole thing by not giving her Jeff's number to begin with, all hell broke loose.

She sent him a text saying that she was canceling the appointment due to, "JB is jealous, insecure and afraid that something might happen between us." She conveniently left out the part about her being attracted to him. Nevertheless, she should never have told him as an outsider her thoughts of whether or not I was jealous or insecure, which I was not.

Speaking negatively against your mate automatically places a wedge between the two of you, therefore your bond is broken or in serious jeopardy of being broken, displaces your loyalty, splits your intimacy and drastically deviates from the required or desirable elements, qualities or characteristics. It's called being in-tune with each other; it's having your souls in harmony. Ladies, if you want a man to love your soul the way you want it to be loved, then you have to love that way yourself.

In any given situation you must put yourself in the other person's shoes. In the previous situation, do you think it was appropriate for Monee' to tell me that she was attracted to Jeff and ask me for his number because she wanted him to train her? Let's go a step further; do you think it was appropriate for me to give her his number? Now let's get really extreme; should I have just shielded her from him and never let them meet at all? Can you imagine what the world would be like if any guy tried to hide his beautiful woman from every attractive guy?

Let's be realistic! The bottom line is we have to establish and maintain a mutual line of loyalty, intimacy, affection and attraction for each other. Anytime you share a personal thought with someone other than your mate, or at least before you've shared that thought with your mate, you are crossing the line and violating an unwritten, yet sacred bond of intimacy. People, it's not that hard! You have to make the decision in your own mind first. There are things that must be followed in a marriage or committed relationship to make it work, otherwise just be by yourself and live the single life.

DISCUSSION QUESTION—WHAT IS INTIMACY TO YOU?

CHAPTER IX

"WHO'S THE MAN"

We have evolved into a crazy, twisted, mixed up world and are forever confusing ourselves more as to God's order. It was not God's design for women to be the head of the house or even to live alone. It is very unfortunate that women already outnumber men statistically, and these numbers are drastically diminished even more because of early death from violence, imprisonment, and homosexuality, then that's compounded with women who can't seem to keep it straight as to who's the man. Let me convey a few thoughts to you in another spoken-word piece.

WHO'S THE MAN?

I'm the man, cause I provide; I'm the man, cause, I decide.

When we travel I guide, open the bible, look inside;

He's the leader, she's the bride; Sometimes I'm shy, I can't deny,

Cause in God's eyes; I'm the man; Who's the man? I'm the man!

Not because of the skin that I'm in Or even the parts that extend

I may be stronger, but I don't always win, I'm not perfect and neither are they

And when I'm down and out I'm never too proud to get down on my knees to pray

And when my Daddy died, in my woman's arms I cried;

Oh yeah, I cried; I didn't hide, all my pride was placed aside.

Cause in God's eyes; I'm the Man.

Loving the soul of a black woman requires that a man completely be a man and a woman completely be a woman, but what exactly does that mean? Some women want so badly to tell a man what to do. Don't get me wrong, I'm not saying that women should never have control over some things, and I'm not talking about sex, but when the subject is a matter of the home or bills you have to take a step back. The man should always discuss the topics with you and take into consideration how you feel, but the final decision rests upon the shoulders of the man.

In order to be the man you have to possess certain qualities that make you the man. Does the type of car a man drives have anything to do with it? Some women have this idea that a man doesn't have status unless he drives a Mercedes, BMW or Lexus. Relax ladies, if the shoe doesn't fit, then don't put it on. I used to drive a Jag when Monee' and I met, but I drove my truck for our first date because I wanted to feel her out to see how she felt about what a man drives.

Although she passed the, "girl, what kind of car does he drive?" test, I sometimes felt that I should have also dressed down and spoke less intelligently; that would have really shown me where her heart was at if she would have kept feeling me.

So what makes up a man's status? When we met I was an adjunct theatre professor and very active with my production business. I have two degrees and a National Emergency Medical Technician license, so why wasn't I the ideal guy? Remember my Pastor friend I told you about earlier?

When he counseled me for marriage he said that unions are not 50/50 but 100/100, which I interpreted to mean that if the man focused 100% of his attention towards pleasing her and the woman focuses 100% of her attention towards pleasing him, then neither of them would ever appear to be selfish or negligent.

It has to be realized and accepted that in a marriage or committed relationship he is you and you are him. Everything that is done represents each other. The very moment that you stop thinking that way is the wake of destruction.

In conversation with Sophia she told me that after 23 years of marriage to Karon she is really tired of some of his short-comings and more particularly the way "he" runs "his" business. Wrong choice # 1; it used to be "we" run "our" business. She said "I'm going to step away and let him do everything his own way." Wrong choice # 2.

Immediately, yet subtly I asked her if she realized that she was using individual words like I, my and me, instead of our, we and us? Ladies, it is so easy for you to turn tail and run when the going gets tough. If he loved your soul, then he would know that somewhere in your notions the things that he said or did were driving you to abandon your thoughts of unity, which are reflected by our, we and us. Things can only get so bad and then they will get better.

While you're steadily pointing your finger at him you're forgetting about the commitment you made. I know, I know! "I'm not going to be doing everything if he ain't doing nothing!" I get it, but what you're not getting is as you are attempting to get back at him you're changing who you are. "I can do bad by myself!" I know; that's true, but you have to stay in touch with what makes you whole and complete.

Sophia truly believes in a man being the man, so in her moments of frustration confusion set in and took her mind to the left for a bit. So what, he's not savvy when it comes to business or doing taxes; she is, and that's what makes the union complete.

There are strengths and weaknesses in all of us. I promise you, Sophia, if you look hard enough, as with all of the rest of us, you will find many imperfections in yourself. Karon, you have to go back to chapter 3 and practice up on your listening skills. Additionally, take a gander back at chapter 4 and think about learning what she wants.

Don't take it for granted that she does all of the wonderful things to make you feel like the man, like preparing and serving your meals; I'd like to know how many times have you given her a tip… I have taken a glance inside her car and in a word it's "filthy!" I've also pumped gas in her car; I don't think a woman should ever have to pump gas!

Hold on, Karon, I know you're thinking that you don't know when her car needs gas. "BS!" Here's a tip for all the fellas; your car uses less gas when it's full, so fill it up, and instead of putting $10.00 or $15.00 in every few days to raise just above ¼ of a tank, pretend that ¾ is empty and never let it get lower than that.

You only have to sacrifice filling it up once, then use the same concept of $10.00 or $15.00 every few days; she's worth it! In fact, at least once a week you should check the oil, water, tire pressure, cleanliness and gas; it's called "preventive maintenance." Make it a part of your normal routine.

That won't guarantee that her car will never break down, but at least it will take the apprehension from the forefront of her mind. Eliminating her thoughts of those concerns is anticipating her needs, hence loving her soul.

This goes out to all of the Karons in the world; "she should never have to ask you to take out the trash, fix a leaky faucet, change a blown light, tighten a loose door knob, repair a broken step, oil a squeaky hinge or replace a cabinet door that hanging on by one screw." Fellas, are you getting the picture?

Ladies, back to you, remember chapter 7? **"Don't let the outside in."** He's not just the man of the house; he's the man of your life. When you take the word of outsiders over him, make a deal or form a bond you are inviting trouble inside. Veteran's day, 2012 Monee' had to work and I decided to take advantage of the free meal that various places grant us; I chose Applebee's for my signature medium rare, sirloin and shrimp parmesan cheese steak dinner with a cold glass of raspberry lemon-aide. As I walked in and approached the hostess I saw a female that appeared to look familiar to me. Not quite sure where I recognized her from, I simply said hello and kept it moving. I sat alone and after placing my order, as so many others do, I played with my smartphone while awaiting my meal.

Later that evening Monee' and I got together in keeping with our normal routine. Although I told her where I was going, texted her while there, and shared moments of excitement about the food and service, she launched an inquiry anyway, which immediately aroused my suspicions. She then angrily accused me of being at Applebee's with someone else. I was as confused as I could be because I had no idea what gave her that notion, but it didn't matter because the yelling and swearing was in full effect.

Despite the fact that I adamantly asked what she was talking about and insisted that I ate alone, she continued her intense interrogation. After several threats and many rude comments towards me she finally disclosed that the familiar face that I couldn't recall was Barbara, someone we met at a house party of one of Monee''s friends and saw once more at a birthday party in a local nightclub.

The lying witch called Monee' and told her that I was at Applebee's having dinner with some other woman; the sad part was she believed it to the degree that I caught all the hell from it. I even requested a face to face meeting with Barbara to confront my accuser, as well as a physical description of who she alleged I was with; both requests were denied. I was called a liar, cheat and everything short of a child of God.

Do men lie about that type of thing? Hell yes, all the time! Was I lying? Absolutely not and if I would have been with someone else just suspecting that I knew Barbara was plenty that I wouldn't have been stupid enough to stay. Let me make that situation a little more interesting; Monee' is into "Co-wifing;" she believes that men are created to have up to 4 women or wives.

She used to tell me that I could have other women as long as I told her about it so she wouldn't look like a fool. Armed with that knowledge why the hell would I need to sneak? Furthermore, we barely knew Barbara's lying ass and I was extremely offended by the fact that Monee' believed her over me. I exhausted all of my efforts trying to convince her of my innocence but to no avail.

Ladies, it doesn't make you look like a fool to have trust and confidence in your man, however if you don't trust him it is a lost case; you may as well cut your losses and move on. Your behavior will always be motivated by your suspicious mind. Hold off for a while before wondering if "I" have a mental problem because chapter 10 is going to blow your mind!

By the way, in case you're wondering, I drove a 1999 Mitsubishi Galant, both door handles are broken, the knob on the glove box is damaged and stuck closed, the air conditioner adjustment knob doesn't work properly, there is a hole in the dashboard, the radio doesn't work, the rear window is damaged, the front bumper is taped up, the seats are torn, it burns oil, the carpet is ripped and the air conditioner compressor clicks on and off when the car is idling. Damn right, I'm still driving it and yes I'm a damn good man! Why do I say so confidently that I'm a good man? Is it my infinite wisdom and wealth of knowledge? I will let you decide; just keep reading.

Recently I was in a conversation with a very enthusiastic lady, Morgan, who happens to find me attractive and she began speaking of her long-time relationship with her best friend. She expressed her disappointment that her 20 year confidant doesn't initiate contact as much as she does. Of course the wisdom kicked in and I politely asked if she had a favorite restaurant.

"Yes, I do," she replied with a slight hint of confusion in her voice. "How often do you go?" I continued. "Once or twice a week," she maintained comparatively. "How many times have they come to you?" I craftily asked. "What? They have never come to me." As her curiosity peaked. "When you go there do they shut down and only serve you?" As I neared the end of my line of questioning. "No! Of course not." In her playful reply. "So what do you like about them?" To bring my inquiry to a close." "I like the food, location and the service.

"So they don't do any of that stuff, yet you keep going…" My point being in relationships both parties won't always be equal in communication skills; at least not initiating it, but if you're still getting that same great service, food and the good location, then who cares who calls who the most?"

Just because you refer to someone as your best-friend doesn't always mean that they will consider you to be the same; not that it means they don't like you as much or won't always take your call and enjoy hanging out with you, but they may not be as enthusiastic about being the one who calls first. You can just as easily encounter the same situation in your relationship. You could love to go out bowling, or the movies, but your mate may never be the one to suggest it but always ready to go when you do.

It doesn't mean that he loves any less; you just may be the better communicator with more drive and initiative. We love titles, especially women, and sometimes when we're deprived of those titles we react in a very disappointed way but it's not always a reason to dissolve the relationship. It's my place as a man to share that wisdom because it preserves harmony. As I said in the last chapter, "I love myself some me!"

I told Monee' in the beginning of our relationship that my ultimate mate is a female me; she disagreed and said that is ridiculous. 9 months later after things got really ugly between us she had a change of heart and agreed that having a male version of her would serve to counteract her frustration because he would always love doing the same things as her. He would provide the ultimate understanding of her.

CHAPTER X
"THE WAKE OF DISTRUCTION"

At some point in their life every woman fantasizes about that fairy tale marriage or relationship, but the problem is, they think it will never get out of fantasy land. Of course the whole knight in shining amour is a bit far-fetched but the brother in the shiny BMW is still in reach. Unfortunately what has happened so often is women settle because men are not held to that higher standard.

Don't get me wrong, I know every guy can't afford to buy a BMW, but fellas you don't have to drive one to give your lady that Romeo and Juliette romance. I promise you, if you show her that side of you she will forgive the BEAMER!

There is one other major stressor that we sometimes put in place, which causes big problems. There is a deep rooted anger that black women carry and display when they see a brother with a white woman; especially when that brother is thought of to be a successful one. I have listened to black women complain that a successful black man will go out of his way to find and date the most disgusting and nasty, low-class white woman he can find, while a white man who dates or marries a black woman has to have the most well-dressed, well-spoken, cultured successful pick of the litter.

However, here's some food for thought; it's not always the white man who's looking for that status, it's that type of black woman who seeks out him and feels she won't get the love and treatment she deserves for her accomplishments and status.

Ask yourself if you've ever felt that way. It's funny how some black women seem to be angry because she's black, while others seem to be angry because everyone else isn't. I admire a strong black woman, but there are too many who associates being strong with being loud, rude and feisty towards others.

There's nothing I love more about a woman who is sweet and subtle yet still gets her point across and is able to reach others effectively. Monee' often told me that I was afraid of a strong black woman and that I should get myself a white woman who would be submissive to all my wishes.

It's sad that she never realized just how much admiration I truly have for black women, even though I've dated a few white women in my time. In fact, I was involved with one white woman that damn near cost me my freedom and almost my life; I'll tell you about that later in the chapter.

LESSON 9. "THE TIME TO PREPARE FOR WAR IS IN THE TIME OF PEACE."

Go to hell! As a black man, has any woman ever told you that or have you as a black woman ever said it to someone? What about, f**k you! I hate you! I wish you were dead! Here's a better question: If you were to consider it, going to hell, that is, what additional things would you need to know to accomplish the trip? How far is it?

How long does it take to get there? What do I need to take with me? If I go, can I come back? Smile. Newton's third law suggests that every action has an equal and opposite reaction. We touched on that more in an earlier chapter.

Therefore if a woman tells a man to "go to hell," then you can bet that at some point in the relationship she desired to be in Heaven with him and if she said "f**k you," then she felt that she didn't want to be without him. "I hate you" likely yielded the opposition of her telling him that she loves him, and lastly if she says, "I wish you were dead," then surely she felt that she wanted his love for her to live forever.

I am about to share a few more things with you that will surely make you question my judgment and mental condition, however if you read this book with an open mind and comprehended the philosophy that I've shared, you will know that these experiences have boosted my intellect and strengthened my inner-being. Sure you will gain knowledge from what you have read, but take it from me; nothing teaches you like life experiences. Let's take a common phrase that many of us use every day and reflect how its inappropriate use can lead to calamity.

"I love you" are three of the most powerful words that can be said to a woman; particularly if her love language is "words of affirmation." Fellas, don't ever say it to a woman unless you are more certain than life itself. One night Monee' and I went to a neighborhood bar in my neck of the woods to hang out. It was a quaint little place with a live band, which is an all-time favorite for me. Right from the beginning the conversation was intense and I didn't make it any better with my smart-ass comments and dramatic theatrics. Monee' expressed her views on how someone should respond to a person who they disagreed with and it directly contradicted her own responses.

Thrilled at the fact that I caught her in a lie I began to imitate her, Wrong choice # 1, voice, body language, facial expressions, hand on the hip, neck working, finger snapping and all. Unaware of the topic of our conversation or what preceded my actions, others around us naturally assumed that I was gay and took my actions as such. Monee' immediately rose to her feet, left the table abruptly, and went to the ladies room. A few moments later she exited, paid the tab at the counter then returned to the table to get her coat. She began walking out without speaking to me; only the harsh frown upon her face indicated her mounting anger. I called out to her but my words were ignored as I walked hurriedly behind her. She swiftly bobbed and weaved her way through the crowded club towards the exit as I struggled behind to keep up.

Once we were both in the vehicle the silent treatment continued the saga. Still not realizing that I triggered the whole thing I began voicing my objections to her walking away from me; Wrong choice # 2. She responded with, "I told you I don't like being embarrassed in public! Those guys at the table behind you were making fun of me! They said, "I guess he told you!" Then they snapped their fingers like gays!" Of course my pride kicked in again and I said, "to hell with those guys!" I still didn't acknowledge her growing irritation, then she asked me if I would have a problem with her having a friend come pick her up from my apartment, to which I told her hell yes I would have a problem with it! "Another man is not coming to my house to pick up my lady as a result of you being mad at me behind a disagreement! If you're that pissed off, I'll take you home;" Wrong choice # 3. She flew into a rage and began screaming, "stop this damn car and let me out!" "I will take you home; just relax," I said, as her annoyance intensified even more. "I'm not going anywhere with you!

I'm not playing, Motherf**ker! I will jump out and I don't care if I kill myself!" as she proceeded to open the car door and started yelling out to other drivers. "Somebody help me! This Motherf**ker's kidnapping me!" I reached over and grabbed her coat as one of her legs extended from the moving vehicle and said, "stop it, Monee'! You are going to kill yourself and get me arrested!" "I don't care! God, please strike this faggot-ass man in his head and flip this car so I can get away from him! Please God, I don't care if I die! I just want to get away from his faggot-ass, God!"

I was unable to pull over, so I continued to hold on to her as her struggle to jump out of the car sustained. Then she started chanting in a language that I did not understand. Once I was able to stop safely she sprung out of the car and started walking away briskly into the darkness. I put the car in a safe condition, then went after her and foolishly made the ultimate wrong choice # 4. "Leave me the hell alone, JB! You don't love me! You don't even care about me so just go find you somebody else!" "That's not true; I do love you!" I proclaimed as I position myself in front of her. Immediately her entire demeanor changed as if some type of supernatural power came over her.

She looked at me and asked, "You love me?" "Yes." I replied as I felt the tension ease up and she drew closer to me, then we embraced. "I'm sorry; I didn't mean to embarrass you. Please let me take you home. I can't leave you out here. You can cool down and we can get together tomorrow. She melted into me like a stream of water blending into a river and I walked her slowly back to the car. I took her home and ensured that she was tucked in safely, then went off to head home. I wrongly misused the power of "words of affirmation" to gain an unfair advantage over her, but what I didn't acknowledge was that I caused more harm than good; remember what I said about using those three words inappropriately? The inappropriate thing about it was, the fact that I wasn't in love with her and under those conditions it was certainly not the right time to say it just to calm her down.

Yeah, I know; I'm crazy, I'm stupid and everything else, but don't leave out "smarter." This may sound a bit far-fetched too but I had to do some really deep soul searching of myself over the last few years. I cleansed my mind of every negative thing that I could muster up. I put myself in an extremely bad legal situation back in 2001, after which you could barely get me to spit on the sidewalk from my ferocious apprehension of incarceration. Some guys feel that being the man is all about showing how tough you are and that sometimes includes mistreating women. I was exposed to some harsh conditions growing up and then spent 14 years in the military, but the most challenging test of my manhood was spending the night in jail.

It ultimately resulted from yet another wrong choice and was the most horrifying experience that I ever dealt with in life. I committed a terrible sin; no I didn't murder anyone. I cheated with a married woman, although I was single at the time. Unfortunately we got caught and to save her ass she accused me of rapping her and molesting her child. I was arrested for indecency with a child and spent the night in jail. After I produced some evidence that mitigated the allegations the charges were dismissed. However, angered by the fact that I was on his property without his permission or knowledge, the husband filed criminal trespassing charges and I served a year on probation under deferred adjudication conditions.

Unfortunately for me, due to our screwed up laws the original charge is reflected on my criminal record after 13 years. I developed a tremendous trust complex after that and it paid off because Monee' tried to hit me with the "I'm gonna tell the cops that you raped me" game-plan, which is the opening story of the last chain of occurrences in the book. A recorded phone conversation was my saving grace. Monee's rage and discontent for me manifested so profoundly that she, the same woman who said she loves me more than anything or anyone falsified a 911 call, telling them that I raped her. Remember I told you that she suffers from migraine headaches? She took some prescribed Fioricet pain pills and drank 2 Batch 19 beers behind them, then fell to the floor before I could catch her. As I dashed to her rescue to pick her up, her dog, a little raggedy –ass poodle attacked me and bit my hand.

I didn't want her to fall to the floor again, so I kicked the dog; she came to, briefly enough, to see the action and with her words slurring grossly she cursed me up one side and down the other. "You kicked my dog! He is only 8 pounds! I'm calling 911 and tell them you raped me and kicked my dog!" I attempted to comfort her, as I struggled to move her to the sofa. "Calm yourself down, Monee'; that damned dog bit me while I was trying to pick you up. You almost hit your head on the corner of the computer. Please relax and let me get you to the sofa." "F**k that, liar! He's just 8 pounds! I'm calling them!" she insisted. She called 911 and attempted to tell them that I raped her but her words were so slurred that the operator was unable to determine clearly what was said. Of course the call was recorded.

I convinced Monee' to go with me to the car so I could take her to the police station, so I called the 911 operator back and told her that I was bringing Monee' to the station; she asked me where Monee' was at and I told her that she was passed out in my car, so the operator instructed me to take Monee' back home to my apartment and await an Officer's arrival.

We both arrived at the same time and when Monee' got out of the car she staggered so badly that I had to hold her up and put her inside. The Officer looked at me and said, "Damn, she's wasted! Is she always that wasted this time of day?" "No, we're going through some things and she's been drinking." I admitted. "How much did she have to drink?" He continued, "Two beers,"

I told him as we walked slowly towards the apartment. "Did she have anything else? It's hard to believe that only two beers can do that to someone. She must not be used to drinking." He insisted. "That's all I'm aware of," I lied to prevent her from suffering a closer inspection. "Well, what do you want me to do? Do I need to talk to her?" He asked. "It's up to you." "If you're good, I'm not dealing with this crap. She looks okay to me." He proclaimed as he turned and walked back to his patrol car and pulled away.

I went back inside and was greeted with a blaze of curse words. "Why the hell didn't you let me talk to the cops?" she asked furiously. "That's some bullshit! He can't do that! I called 911! That's why I don't like y'all damn cops! You all stick together! I'm gonna get his ass fired! I'm calling his supervisor!" She called the 911 operator back and insisted on speaking with the supervisor. I left and according to her the supervisor agreed to meet with her later in the evening. To my knowledge that never happened.

Somehow we managed to get past that episode, but it didn't get any better; so on to the next one. The drinking and taking pills continued to the point that she went to a local bar to support her bad habit. One night while at the bar she got high and texted me; at the same time she was reaching out to her sister who agreed to go pick her up, but I got there first.

Upon arrival she was very belligerent towards me; her sister insisted that she put me on the phone to confirm that she was not leaving with a stranger. As she was passing me the phone it missed my hand, fell to the floor and broke apart. It was on! "You broke my phone, Motherf**ker!" She started pushing me and took a swing. I merely restrained her to keep her from striking me, but an unaware asshole next to us waved for security.

Security approached, confronted me and said, "Hey! Hey, we don't need no trouble in here, man!" I replied, "I'm not causing trouble." He then said, "you were in here last week and you and her was going at it. Y'all need to keep all that at the house." I took up a defensive posture and said, "hey dude, do I look intoxicated to you? I'm only here to take her home. She's high."

After a closer look at Monee' he changed his position and began speaking more cordial to me. "I didn't realize that, man." Monee' said, "f**k this and walked towards the bathroom. The security officer and I exchanged numbers and he said that he was cutting her off and asking her to leave for the night. When she returned she immediately lit in on me. "Why the hell is he still here, Officer?" "He's here to take care of you, Ma'am." He replied.

"I don't need him to take care of me!" she said angrily. "Look, he's gonna take you home; I don't come between family." Security insisted. "He ain't my family! I'm stuck! He ain't shit! Why are you even listening to his stripe shirt wearing ass?" She continued.

"Don't let him intimidate you! Look how big you are and how little he is! You can kick his ass! Y'all are a damn trip; letting this little Motherf**ka scare y'all!" "Ma'am, it's not about all that. We just wanna make sure that you're safe, that's all." He said. "Then you take me home... I don't wanna go nowhere with him!" Why are you kicking me out anyway?" she asked. "I think you've had enough." He explained. "I'm good! I haven't had that much! I know how much I can drink before getting drunk!" she said. "What's your limit?" he asked. "two-Three beers." She confessed.

"And how many have you had?" he continued. "Just one pitcher! That's all!" she revealed. "Ma'am, a pitcher is 6 beers, so you've already had twice your limit; just go home and you can come back in a couple of days. I'm not banding you; just asking you to go home tonight." He concluded.

Her brother in-law arrived in a tow truck to pick up her vehicle and take her to their home, so I went outside to greet him. Moments later she came outside in a rage yelling and pleading with him to not take her vehicle because it would cost $75.00 per day to store. She didn't even recognize him. I assisted her into the truck as she continued to cry and beg him not to take her vehicle.

I tried to calm her and explain who he was but she flew into yet another rage and started punching the dashboard, then physically attacked me; another security officer who was unaware what was going on came to her rescue and approached me. Again I had to explain to him who I was and what the situation was. She began pleading with him until he left, then continued screaming and crying until she passed out on the front seat.

I elected to go home and let her family take care of her for the night. I received a call the next morning saying that she had another seizure and was en route to the hospital. I met them there and after a short stint in the hospital, yep you guessed it I took her home with me. I endured a few more attacks in the coming weeks.

One morning at about 3:15 she snatched my blanket off and started cursing, punching and stomping on it. Saying that it was ridiculous for a grown-ass man to be attached to a blanket and that it's all my blanket's fault that she and I were not sleeping closely nor having sex as frequently anymore. A few nights later she denied me access to my own car by withholding the key and I was late to a meeting, so I took my truck.

She cursed me out publicly at least three more times, and then finally when the attacks became infinitely physical to my person I had to involve the police. Sunday, October 27th 2013 was the last straw. I fell asleep in the front room recliner. When I awoke I went into the bathroom to brush my teeth and the noise startled her.

She walked through the apartment calling out to her dog. As she walked right past me I thought she was joking, so I stood quietly. Wrong choice # 1; Once she discovered that it was me she instantly became pissed off. "You knew I was scared and you didn't say nothing! Since you want to sleep in the damn living-room, then you can give me my damn money! Give me my money right now!" "I don't have any money, Monee'." I proclaimed as she lunged towards me.

At 4:22 a.m. she yanked my blanket once again and took it to the kitchen, threw it on the floor, open the refrigerator, took out lemon-aid, chocolate syrup, cocktail sauce and honey mustard and commenced pouring it on the blanket. I left the apartment and called the police.

Upon the arrival of the police, Monee had already plotted a plan to take all of my personal hygiene items and hide them from me, so she manipulated an officer to help her unknowingly put "my" suitcase filled with everything from deodorant to hair clippers in her vehicle.

After a call from the 911 operator, I returned to the apartment and went inside as they began their questioning. She boldly told the officers that the syrup got on the blanket from kinky sex and I called them because she had enough and ask me to stop, but I didn't, so I got mad and called 911. "A lot of sense that made, right?"

She then jeopardized her position by telling them that I used to be one of them, so I know how to talk and what to say to them; they immediately flanked her and asked me what I wanted them to do. I simply asked them to run interference until I got my stuff to get the hell out of there. They asked me whose name was on the lease and how long had she been living there.

The lease was in my name but since she had been living there more than 30 days that I would have to evict her, so the best thing for me to do was just leave and I did. I've been homeless since that day. In an attempt to reconcile our relationship she sent me a series of text messages that varied in intensity and reflected her bipolar behavior.

LESSON 10. "FAST IS TOO FURIOUS."

What you are about to read are actual messages; or are they? You decide! I've heard it said many times that "This stuff is too real to be fiction! You can't make this up!" I'll leave it up to you... You will have to figure out if the misspelled words and bad grammar are true or false.

To Me
Nov 3 at 4:20 PM

```
This message was sent from a T-Mobile
wireless phone.
Aaaaaaaaaaaaah!!!!!!!!!!:-) I left u a
voicemail!
Have a great day! My power is back! I
have love now... Thanks for releasing
me JB. I will always love u and help u
as a friend. Call me anytime u like. I
will listen and respect you as a
friend. I will never back stab or talk
negative behind your back from this
point on. If I have you have it and I
mean it!!! As people I believe we must
help our brothers and sisters out of
this hell hold that the united states
have us in.
```

To Me
Nov 3 at 4:27 PM

```
This message was sent from a T-Mobile
wireless phone.
I hate u JB. I hate the way u was not
man enough to fix this financial
situation first. I hate all of u even
```

your dick. I never want it to touch me
again. NEVER!!!!!!!!!!!!!!!!!!!!!!!!

To Me
Nov 4 at 3:50 PM
This message was sent from a T-Mobile
wireless phone.
And call or text your son and say
goodnight to your grandson. Call ur
grandson start making that a habit.
Read him a bedtime story then he will
be excited and waiting on your call at
night before he goes to bed. So tonight
when u call your grandson ask his mom
is that ok maybe obligate 3 days out
the week to read him a bedtime story.
He will love it and it will be a great
way to bond with him!!

To Me
Nov 4 at 3:51 PM

This message was sent from a T-Mobile
wireless phone.
And call or text your son and say
goodnight to your grandson. Call your
grandson start making that a habit.
Read him a bedtime story then he will
be excited and waiting on your call at
night before he goes to bed. So tonight
when u call ire grandson ask him mom is
that ok maybe obligate 3 days out the
week to read him a bedtime story. He
will love it and it will be a great way
to bond with him!!

To Me

Nov 6 at 4:18 PM

This message was sent from a T-Mobile
wireless phone.
My homeboy will stay in the apartment
today with his Pitbull dog because I
just don't trust you. You keep sneaking
back to Atlanta. Kenney and his boys
took pictures of u and another person
yesterday over here when u got Ur car
so I don't trust you at all. So i have
my homeboy posted up here only to
protect my belongings. U r very
dangerous and I am afraid of u. I'm
takin a restraining order out on u due
to u sneaking back and forward from the
apartment when u think I'm not here and
u lied about returning the keys. I
don't want u anymore I have moved on. I
don't understand y u keep driving back
and forth waiting gas money. I don't
love or have like for u anymore.

To Me
Nov 8 at 4:16 PM

This message was sent from a T-Mobile
wireless phone.
If there is anything I could do that
can help make your life easier then I
will. I am a women of my words. And
money is to be shared to help other not
to be saved in a bank to accumulate
tax. I am so grateful from the bottom
of my heart to have shared 14 months of
learning with you. The session is over
and I have took the best lesson of all

with me! Which is the cell in your body reacts to everything your mind says. Negativity brings down your immune system. I have love n contentment and I know what peace is. I have been on both side now. Negative (non-peace) vs positive (peace) and peace is the best side to be on. As the spirits guide me to my destinations. I am sooooooo happy and free my butterfly has wings. I know you're sleep u can call me later!!!!!!!

To Me
Nov 15 at 12:45 AM

This message was sent from a T-Mobile wireless phone.
Hey JB this is something u should consider to put in your journal or on your wall notes. This is and will be the answer to your problem. Just believe me your friend Monee'. Though prayer we birth in God's vision for our lives, which require your body to adapt to the growth taking place inside you, our spiritual bodies have to adapt to the purpose, destiny and vision God has planted in us. This can only be done through a life of prayer, without it you leave yourself open for satanic attacks. So stop running and quitting JB, Go back to your roots JB, Go back and put God in your life! That is the first thing u need to Finnish... U left the church a long time ago... U never finished giving God all of u!!! That is and will be the answer to resolving

your problem.
Your friend Monee' :-)

To Me
Nov 27 at 12:42 AM

This message was sent from a T-Mobile
wireless phone.
Dear Ms. Monee'
This message is to officially inform u
that I am ceasing all ties and
communication with u. As a result of
vacating the residence in Smyrna, we
have both been removed from renters
insurance and you r removed from
vehicle insurance effective Friday Nov
29th. Your number has been blocked and
I humbly request that you cease all
communication with me as well. Your CPR
cards were mailed to your business as I
said they would be. I have turned in
all keys of 2025F to the front office.
Any further attempts by you to
communicate with me will be taken as
aggressive and a threat towards me. I
truly wish you well and pray that you
are blessed in all that you do. I pray
that God shines his light on you and
urge you to just walk away and accept
what has come to be. I do not wish you
any bad luck and I harbor no ill
feelings. Take care,
Jb

Monee' went on to call my apartment complex office and
tell them that I was selling prostitutes from my apartment,

call my job and tell them that I was going to kill her and sent an inflammatory text to my family, friends and coworkers. The following text message with my picture attached was sent out in mass on Thanksgiving morning.

To Me
Nov 28 at 12:30 AM

This message was sent from a T-Mobile wireless phone. Warning !!! Let play pass this email and text. This man ostensibly a con artist he robs females and charm them and have a rule that all black women has attitude. When u meet him he will tell you to do two things for him be kind and sexually please him. He has a thing for young girls. And a case that was dismissed in regard of a young girl. He dresses to impress but he is broke. He don't have any money. He will make you pay for everything because he believes he is a celebrity. He keeps a sharp cut but don't let this fool you because this is a true co artist. He keeps a sharp cut to get the educated women to pray on. He will slam you with his broke down business idea that is never going to work. He does not make any money from JB star production. However he will make you believe that the business will make money. He will come in your life and charm you out of your money. I have witness that is ready to talk about how this con artist owes them money. He has a great way with words so be careful. This email and text is to warm females of him. He has co me out of 15 thousand dollars in a total of 14 months. He is also a control freak and will put his hand on you if necessary. He wears a cross around his neck and carries and unregistered gun. He drives a Mitsubishi black car with dinks on the hood and a white Chevy truck with a cab on the back. His apartment is 2025F lake-park Dr. Smyna GA 30080. He is currently desperate for money so he is letting karaz use his apartment for a escort business so he could pay his rent by December 1st,

2013. He will fool you with his dress and always talk about JB star production. Which you could look up on YouTube. Any other info you need please text me i have a private Facebook that have other info regarding this co artist. It private so we will have to screen you for you to going. Also this part is a rumor that he may like men too. And beware!!!!!

She accused me of emailing some nude pictures of her out on the internet and it was a part of the charges she was bringing against me for my arrest. The following text message was sent to my phone as a threat to intimidate me regarding the court date.

To Me
Nov 28 at 4:07 PM

This message was sent from a T-Mobile wireless phone. 3 more police reports has been made and 3 complaints at G4S at 1370 Browning Rd
Center Point 5 Suite 10 Columbia, SC: We have 3 case #, 1-800-307-9005
Court for the two children that open the pornographic email is on Monday. Charges are being presses. I guess u was hopping for people to be made at me however that are going to arrest u. We have proof of the email ip address and the investigator gave the police that info. Please think so u won't lose urn job and go to jail. A lot of those email addresses is kids so they are openings your pornographic emails.

December 16th 2013 we went to court to face her accusations against me and this written transcript of a recorded conversation between us with Monee' plotting to lie to the police about me rapping her was my saving; the funny thing about it was I completely forgot that she put the recorder on my phone. I was cleaning up my phone one night and discovered the conversation. I allowed her to sink deeper and deeper with her lies in court. She wrote the following affidavit declaring my threats towards her.

In court she told the judge that I threatened her in person by saying that if she didn't give me $1,500.00 that I would blow her head off. She openly admitted to sending out the text about me, which is clearly defamation of character and she lied and was caught about who took the nude pictures of her and how they were distributed.

As soon as the judge listened to the phone conversation he immediately pulled the plug on the whole thing and dismissed her case. The language is harsh and the grammar is bad, but you have to decide for yourself how much of it is actually true and how much is fiction.

CAUTION! EXTREMELY EXPLICITE

Brown… Yeah

Monee'… did you just put me on hold?

Brown… God, I'm so sick of this shit! Please leave me alone. I'm begging you.

Monee'… Did you just put me on hold?

Brown… Just walk away; do the friend thing; I'm with you now; you've convinced me. Do the friend thing and everything cool.

Monee'… What street are you on?

Brown… Over; I don't know what street I'm on.

Monee'… Well look up and look at the FUCKIN SIGN!

Brown… go handle your business and leave me alone. I'm fine.

Monee'… Alright! Alright! I will handle my business! I'm gonna park my truck behind your car; you're not gonna be able to move it. And I, and I, and I, **I WANT YOU TO CALL THE COPS ON ME! I'M GONNA TELL THEIR ASS THAT YOU RAPE ME LAST NIGHT! I GOT YOUR CUM IN ME! I'M GONNA TELL THEM I WAS AFRAID TO TELL! I WENT TO THE HOSPITAL; I'M ON THIS MEDICINE! IT MESSED UP MY RIGHT FRAME OF THINKING; HE TOOK ADVANTAGE OF ME! THAT'S EXACTLY WHAT I'M GONNA TELL THEM! I'M GONNA TELL THEM HE PUT HIS GUN TO MY FUCKIN HEAD! HIS GUN IS IN THE BACK SEAT OF HIS CAR OR TRUNK! OFFICER IF YOU DON'T BELIEVE ME IT'S ILLEGAL!** I ASKED YOU TO TELL WHERE YOU'RE AT!

Brown… And I asked you to leave me alone.

Monee'… AND I ASKED YOU TO TELL ME WHERE THE FUCK YOU AT! NEGRO!

Brown… I'm a grown ass man and that's what I'm doing.

Monee'… If I tried this shit, I'm doing something, so when you see that house, Negro, I'll be right there. I'm so sick of this shit!

Brown… Then leave me alone.

Monee'… I'm so sick of you, jb! I'M GONNA WHIP THE FUCK OUTTA YOUR ASS! AND I'MMA SIT IN JAIL! AND WHEN PEOPLE ASK ME WHY I'M IN JAIL I'M GONNA TELL THEM CAUSE I BEAT THE FUCK OUT OF MY MAN! HIS PUSSY-ASS NEEDED A WHIPPING! **CAUSE HE WON'T LET HIS WOMAN HELP HIM!** This is all your fault, if you had gotten my medicine last night I would have been straight okay.

Brown… That's fine, I'm…

Monee'… You lied to me and told me you would go get my medicine this morning; you got me all off balance; I been on a regiment; you get me at your house and get me all off balance knowing that you didn't have no intentions to go get that medicine; you knew you wasn't gonna get up because I'm not somebody else who you get up on time for! And now you're telling me you're walking home when you know that little ugly ass, skinny ass, stupid bitch probably coming to pick you up! I'm gonna wait on her ass too! She gone get beat the fuck down when she pull up at your apartment! I'm telling you now! Where are you at? I'm not playing with your ass! That's what's wrong with you! You need a woman to put your ass in check, you get to do whatever you wanna do! Where are you at?

Brown… Don't worry;

Monee'… Oh believe me, negro, I'm gonna worry about that shit cause I'm gonna finish this! I'm gonna finish this today! JB, I'm gonna tell you one more time; where are you at? **You need to turn your recorder on cause I'm bout to fuck your apartment up!** You don't tell me where you're at; I don't care!

Brown… Don't do nothing like that.

Monee'… I'm about to knock everything out! I'm about to bust your fuckin windows out your car!

Brown… I'm fine.

Monee'… I ain't one of those women who just, I ain't one of those women who just, you gonna do whatever the fuck you wanna do and you don't get checked about it! Let's see, you don't wanna tell me? I'll be at your apartment waiting on your motherfuckin' ass! I got the key to your fuckin' car too! I'm gonna drive that fuckin' bitch off! I'm gonna get there before you! You're gonna see my truck and you're gonna see your car gone! **And you better record this shit**! Cause I'm gonna park that bitch and you ain't gonna be able to find it! And I'm gonna walk back and I'm gonna get my car! You want drama?

You gone get drama cause I ask you nicely where you at; you won't tell me where you at! If I did this shit, you would've been screaming your head off and not let me doggone walk, but you get to do this shit; you get to do everything you wanna do, cause I'm bout to act a fool at your apartment! I don't care if you call the fuckin' cops; I don't care! I told your ass to tell me where you at; you don't want to? Okay! I know you're sitting at some gas station waiting for that little bitch to pick you up! That bitch better drop you off by Target! Cause if that bitch come up in your apartment she gonna get her ass whipped! I'm telling you now!

Brown… Go home; go take care of your business.

Monee'… You've been a jinx to me with this money shit! The more money I make the more you try to jinx it cause you're jealous cause you can't make money! And I try to help your broke ass and you don't want nobody to help you! You wanna hang with all the broke people! You don't want your rent paid next month it's fine with me! It's fine with me! You want drama it's fine with me! I'll be at your house in five minutes! Five minutes! Look at you, walking with fuckin' dressy ass shoes on! You fucked up my day and you're trying to make like I fucked up your day. You lied to me.

Brown… I don't care.

Monee'… Alright. Okay. I'm glad you don't care. I'm telling you. I'm tired; I'm tired of your ass! You're always fuckin' shit up! Did anybody ever tell you you're a fuck up? I'm trying to help you not be a fuck up! I try to give you the confidence; I try to give you the confidence! I tell your ass to go hunt for them cards! I tell you to give me the business cards! All your friends are losers! Even Shacoo is a loser! He won't even help your ass out!

Brown… Yep. You're right.

Monee'… And I'm asking you to let me help your ass out and your ass still won't accept the fuckin' help! I don't even need this fuckin' check! JB, I'm gonna calm the fuck down, where the fuck are you? I need to get my medicine! Where the fuck are you? Where are you at, JB?

Brown… I'm walking my fat ass home, so please leave me alone; I'm asking you as nicely as I can.

Monee'… I'm not! You don't tell me what the fuck to do at this point cause you're not in the right fuckin' frame of mind! Your ass needs help! Your ass need help and you don't wanna accept the fuckin' help and you wanna hang out with fuckin' loser and I'm trying to get these fuckin' losers out your life! I'm trying to tell you everything but your fuckin' ass don't wanna listen to me! Where are you at so I can come get your ass!

Brown… I don't need you to come get me. I'm fine; I need to walk.

Monee'… Where are you at?

Brown… My fat ass needs to walk.

********* END RECORDING *********

After I left, a few weeks later Monee' and I met up following what you just read and prior to her taking me to court. Her appearance had change dramatically and my heart felt it every moment that I was there with her. I started talking about the grief and relief I felt from being away from her and my burning desire to reconnect with my family.

It was strange that I actually still found comfort in talking to her. She started crying and oddly without thinking it through I reach out to comfort her and she exploded, "Don't touch me! Don't be trying to comfort me!" She yelled as my constant attempts to console her by rubbing her shoulders were rejected.

"You're the one who I'm hurting over! What makes you think I want you to comfort me, unless you were gonna take me back? She continued. "I'm not like you! I'm not over you, jb! Maybe this shit is easy for you, but it ain't for me! She confessed as the tears streamed profusely from her eyes. "Don't touch me! I hate you! Don't ever touch me again! Maybe later when I'm over you we can be friends…"

Then the strangest thing that I ever encountered happened; it was like an out of body experience. Suddenly I felt encircled like everything was closing in and all I could see and hear were visions of her and flashes of her voice from the last 14 months. All of the nasty, ugly and rude things that had happened between us began to unfold in my mind as though released from being blocked out.

It was at that moment "my" soul finally realized and accepted that our relationship was demolished; our lives were torn; we were in the wake of destruction. I stayed in denial for over a year; my soul was convinced, psychologically, that no matter what happened between us, I would be there and my love for her would not change.

Please don't get me wrong, loving someone's soul is a beautiful thing; perhaps the most euphoric feeling that you can attain. The key is to ensure that the soul you love is the soul that's meant for you. "**I didn't give Monee' back what she was worth**". Her medical conditions and anger issues did not warrant her not being loved the right way; just by the right person. Ensuring that it's the right person can be a very difficult undertaking sometimes because of the multitude of outside influences; friends, family, peers, coworkers, media, social networking, you get the picture!

I now have a restraining order against Monee' that orders her to stay away from me and my family; she can have no contact by any means, she is ordered to attend family violence counseling and surrender all weapons to the county court for safe keeping for the duration of the restraining order of one year.

However, in good conscience, I must admit, I had to physically leave Atlanta and force myself to stay away from her, otherwise after the dust had settled, tempers stopped flaring, allegations stopped flying and name calling stopped, I feel strongly that we would have gravitated back towards each other yet again because through it all, I still loved her. The soul of her reminded me so much of Wakina that it was freaky scary, and found myself feeling sorry for her and her children.

Not once in 14 months of being together did her children ever dishonor me, talk back, misbehaved or stepped out of line. Okay, now you can say he's crazy! Maybe I am, but the old me didn't tolerate very much at all. As soon as I saw signs of BS I was out. Again, you don't know what you know until you know it. When we left court my friends and family said, "we won! I can't help but wonder if anyone really wins in a situation like this. Both our lives have been altered and there's no turning back; no words, no explanations, no apologies…

I needed to know what my limits were. I am sending out a sincere generic apology to Monee' and every other woman that I held a short-term relationship with. Likewise, I'm sending out a sincere apology to the gentleman that I grossly dishonored by engaging in sex with his wife. I was wrong and I pray that the damage caused by my actions has somehow been repaired over the last thirteen years since this happened.

It is said that Cancers love hard, but what I've discovered through this experience is, for me loving someone's soul is extremely compelling and you can easily get in way too deep because it can make you lose focus due to the blind acceptance of their actions, which is an incompatible task within itself. I used to be a hardcore surface lover and would never allow myself to love that deeply.

That is to say that I was strictly superficial; females are exposed at a very early age to the effects that the development of their bodies have on males. The breasts enlarge, the hips protrude, the thighs tone up causing the baby fat to go away and the waistline seems to shrink as the tummy flattens. As they continue to grow older they become more familiar with how easy it is to get their way just by how they look and the way they smile, but not going all the way. Females have an innate sense of knowledge about safe guarding their temples.

I have met several women who have introduced their "wait for sex" rule to me. I've gotten every time span from 1 month to 6 months to until marriage. If a woman truly desires for a man to love her soul and a man honestly wants to reciprocate, then he will honor her request to wait, but the focus shouldn't be on the time frame but on the mutuality that should develop when they "both" are ready to proceed.

There is no logic to give yourself a sense of obligation to a time frame if your souls are aligned; you could reach the given deadline and he not be ready or she can become ready prior to the expiration of her prescribed time.

With the divorce rate being as high as it is today, fewer marriages and relationship are breaching the 25-50 year mark. Society plays a major role in the development of that mindset. Many older single women trying to compete in today's society are starting off on the wrong foot when they meet a man; for example I met a 45 year old lady in Church.

There was an obvious immediate physical attraction, but I detected within the first 5 minutes of conversation that we would not even reach the point to consider a love connection because of 2 questions she asked me. The first was, "What's your occupation?" After a 20 minute conversation the second question was "What's your number?" A woman in her 40's who is interested in a man will give him her phone number because of her "old school" mentality, then the exchange of occupational information will come later during conversation; not as a direct blunt question.

I'm blessed, however because through my experience with Monee' now I know how to love sensibly, regulate that love by regulating myself, and anticipating the needs, desires and most importantly the thoughts and actions of a woman, hence properly loving the soul of a black or any woman.

DISCUSSION QUESTION—BASED ON THE BOOK'S PHILOSOPHY DO YOU BELIEVE THAT YOU LOVE YOUR MATE'S SOUL?

D. Jerome Brown 22

www.ingramcontent.com/pod-product-compliance
Lightning Source LLC
Chambersburg PA
CBHW060306290526
45789CB00001B/423